Accidental Agent

Accidental Agent

JOHN GOLDSMITH

Charles Scribner's Sons • New York

The author before his first
mission

The author after his first
mission

Leonetti

Bartoli (taken in 1961)

Pierre-Michel, from a
war-time identity card

Pierre-Michel, Cannes,
1970

Introduction

Have you ever felt that your memory is playing tricks on you? I began to have that feeling a few months ago when watching yet another of the never-ending T.V. films about a British agent in Nazi-occupied France during the war.

I couldn't remember drinking interminable cups of coffee in gay cafés. It was like gold dust, surely. Wine too. That was on the ration – when you could get it. Wasn't it? As for the casual handing-over of secret messages in the street, that wasn't in the training manuals of Special Operations Executive in my day. Or was it? One thing in particular rang false – the apparent universal comradeship of Resistance fighters throughout France and their undivided loyalty to General de Gaulle. Even after twenty-five years I couldn't swallow that.

I began to look up the many books that have been written on the subject. I checked old correspondence. And memories that had lain buried under a quarter of a century devoted to training racehorses came reluctantly to life, not all of them pleasant ones. I jotted down one or two notes and finally, after I retired from racing, I went back on a trail that had been cold since the war ended.

I even persuaded Bill Moore, a hardened Fleet Street journalist, specializing in investigation, to help my research and dragged him protesting around the back streets of Paris and the dusty lanes of Provence. The result: I was satisfied that those sometimes humdrum, sometimes desperate, hungry and cruel days were fact. The celluloid world of the T.V. screen was mainly fiction. After listening to me pontificate for the umpteenth time Bill Moore said: 'Everyone else has written a book about it. Why don't you? Then we can all have some peace.'

This, then, is the result, a result that would never have been achieved, without the unfailing and untiring help and guidance of Bill Moore, to whom much of the credit is due.

JOHN GOLDSMITH

August 1970

The author returns, in 1970, to the hotel from
which he escaped in 1943.

above: The ledge along which he climbed.
below: Standing by the pillar behind which he hid.

1

O N a scorching day in August 1944 I found myself crouching under the shade of a withered olive tree on the parched slopes of Mont Ventoux about thirty miles or so from Avignon. For once the sky of Provence was not its renowned clear blue. At least not over the mountain, which was shrouded in a dirty brown haze that smelled of charred twigs, cordite, melting rubber and dust – lots of dust. In my imagination it seemed to reek of Germans too, a sour odour of sweaty tunics and stale cigars. As, at that moment, they were cascading down the hillside, in terror-stricken flight, this was hardly surprising. Had I been on their side I would have run too. From my position on a little ridge I could see the maquis scrambling purposefully after the fleeing Master Race. Mixed up with the hard shouts of the Germans came the excited jabbering of victorious Frenchmen. From time to time, as a Nazi group was cornered in the narrow ravine of the sunken road down which they were retreating, the steady crack of rifles accelerated to a fusillade, followed by prolonged bursts of automatic fire, yells, screams and the occasional boom of a grenade. Grenades, I had just discovered, were highly effective in this form of combat. Among the maquisards, or Resistance fighters, crouching near me in the thorny bushes, was a youngster wearing an ancient steel helmet that could have belonged to his grandfather. He was handling a Sten gun with impressive efficiency. Behind him squatted two swarthy peasants, in shirt sleeves, who fired long rifles every few minutes and, by some miracle, talked and smoked incessantly at the same time.

The appearance of a blond young German, stumbling over an ammunition box at a bend in the road a few yards away, silenced them momentarily. He was clutching a bloodstained arm.

Following him came another German who had shed his equipment and carried a dirty white handkerchief in one hand. He was very frightened and seemed to be trying to say something. What it was I never knew. The boy in the old steel helmet walked over to the edge of the road and with only a slight tensing of the muscles of his thin face to indicate his feelings, fired two short bursts from the hip in copybook fashion according to the training manual. The bullets caught the wounded man in the chest and flung him against the bank. He slid to the ground dead. The other German staggered back a few steps and collapsed on his back groaning. One of the peasants walked over, held out his rifle in one hand so that he could reach him better and shot him in the head. The groans stopped. The peasants resumed their talking and smoking and their ruthless young leader waited coolly for his next victim.

As a British officer it was my duty to prevent unarmed prisoners being shot down in cold blood. I did not like or approve of what I saw. I could not bring myself to do it. Yet to have attempted to stop Germans being executed would have been impossible. The battle fought by the maquis of the Vaucluse region was the culmination of everything I had worked for since I joined Britain's Special Operations Executive.

That it should be conducted mercilessly was inevitable.

*　　*　　*

Almost from the moment that France fell, Allied leaders began to plan the creation of a secret army that would be ready to go into action when the opportunity arose to invade the Continent. They had already seen how effective the Fifth Column had been in furthering German aspirations. Now it was to be their turn. Bold and dramatic though this conception was, implementing it proved to be complicated, difficult and trying. For a start, no ready-made organization existed to undertake such a task. One had to be created. In the event, it was Special Operations Executive which came into being in July 1940 with Hugh Dalton, the Minister of Economic Warfare, as its titular chief. According to M. R. D. Foot's book *S.O.E. in France*, Churchill's instruction to Dalton after the birth of the organization was 'And now set Europe ablaze.' What Dalton was to use for matches he did not specify.

S.O.E. had to be started from scratch and the men who controlled it had to learn the job as they went along. It was not an organization like the Secret Service, with a long tradition, sophisticated equipment and highly trained personnel. The military intelligence departments went their own way and did a different job. S.O.E. had the apparently simple objective of keeping alive the spirit of resistance and of recruiting cadre forces on which a secret army could be built. Although regular officers were seconded to it, the organization did not find favour in the eyes of many conventional generals and politicians who regarded orthodox tactics as being more likely to produce conclusive results. The idea of bands of brigands roaming the back areas behind the enemy lines was abhorrent to most of the professional soldiers.

Others, conversely, expected too much of S.O.E., assuming that because a country was occupied its people would be only too pleased to work against the invader. This did not necessarily follow and anyone who thinks that all opponents of the Nazis automatically banded together against a common enemy is sadly mistaken.

Many Britons, even today, have the impression that the French maquis was a national guerilla army with groups working hand in glove from Marseilles to Metz and from Calais to Cannes. Nothing could be farther from the truth. Up to the time the Germans were finally kicked out, factions within the broad frame of the Resistance quarrelled with each other almost as much as with the enemy, while their attitude to the British and Americans, and the Free French Forces for that matter, varied from cautious co-operation to downright distrust and open hostility. It was into this atmosphere of dissension that the first agents of the French section of S.O.E. were plunged. From their reports, often conflicting, policies had to be evolved; training schemes had to be produced; lessons had to be learned.

As I have pointed out, S.O.E. did not employ professional spies. Its men and women were amateurs, normally recruited like myself because of their specialist knowledge of the country involved and in particular because of their language qualifications. They came from all walks of life and had a tremendous variety of backgrounds. Not all of them proved to be suited to the tasks that faced them. Even allowing for the fact that there was an urgent need for agents and that the organization was untried, the selection of some of the men sent to France completely baffled me. One or two never ought to have been allowed to set foot in the country not only for their own safety but for the safety of others. A vulnerable agent is worse than no agent at all.

My own experience began in 1942 with the first of my three missions to France. Then, as on subsequent occasions, I was concerned mainly with the establishment of a secret army. To help achieve this I was sent to the South of France to persuade maquis leaders with differing political aims that they could have whatever arms, clothes and money they needed, as long as they united to operate against the Germans when called on. I had to convince them there would be no strings attached and that it was not some devious British plot. That I was able to carry out my orders was due to two factors. The first was that I worked directly with Commandant Pierre-Michel Rayon, one of the most remarkable Resistance leaders of the war. The second was the reliability of the North African section of S.O.E., code name Massingham, in meeting my demands for supplies. Massingham has been much abused as being inefficient in packing ammunition, dropping it haphazardly and having slack administration. I can say only that I had but to ask and I would be up to my neck in containers stuffed with Sten guns, grenades and other weapons of war. Had this not been so the battle on Mont Ventoux could never have been fought.

I went into action that day in the uniform of a major in the Royal Armoured Corps. I had preserved my battledress specially for the occasion and thought it only right that the British army should be represented in Commandant Rayon's personal combat group. No quarter was given that day. No prisoners were taken; the enemy wounded were dispatched where they lay. The memory of the S.S. massacre in the Vercors, fifty miles or so to the north when the local Resistance were butchered after a pitched battle they should never have attempted, was too fresh in everyone's minds. Furthermore, the maquisards of the Vaucluse had held themselves in check for a considerable time, a miracle of self-discipline inspired by Commandant Rayon. When the promised time for a showdown arrived there was no holding them. The pent-up frustrations of years of suffering, injustice, hunger and humiliation exploded in a relentless fury. When the German column which Rayon had lured into a trap turned and fled, the fury engulfed them. At least two hundred and fifty German dead were counted on the slopes of Mont Ventoux. If there were any wounded, I did not see them or hear of them. Our casualty roll amounted to one man, a solitary maquisard who shot off the tip of his finger in the excitement. This, to me, was the final proof of Rayon's claim to be a master of guerilla warfare. In the north, after the D-Day landings, many of the maquis leaders had called out their men prematurely. All control was lost. As a result, although they did widespread damage and seriously interfered with enemy communications, hundreds of lives were squandered needlessly. Had the maquis stuck to the phased plan of operations originally agreed, the same effect could have been achieved at a fraction of the cost in blood.

The fact that not one of the men to whom I supplied weapons was killed on that hot August day was a source of considerable personal satisfaction. The casualty lists that had accumulated on the way were already too long. They were filled with men who would have envied my participation in the battle, S.O.E. agents who had prayed during the years of stealth, sabotage and subversion that one day they would be able to put on uniform and face their enemy in the open. Instead, many of them ended their lives in rags in the execution yards of Himmler's unspeakable prisons. For their sakes alone I am glad that S.O.E. was represented by a man in khaki the day the Germans were broken on Mont Ventoux.

2

I T is very irritating to be excluded from a war, especially when you feel that you have twice as many reasons as anyone else for getting involved. My arguments about double involvement certainly cut no ice with the recruiting sergeant in the R.A.F. offices at Reading, however. Unimpressed by my claim that my French upbringing and English birthright conferred special privileges on me, he gazed bleakly from where he sat at a scrubbed deal table, and said 'Look mate, to start with the Frogs have all the blokes they want in their bloody great air force so they won't want you. And to finish with we only want young men. So do us all a favour. Go home. If we want you we'll send for you. Now then, next please.'

I could hardly contain my frustration and rage as I shouldered my way to the door past a small queue of fresh-faced youths who regarded me with an undisguised mixture of pity and contempt. Too old at thirty-one! It was an insult. Well, I said to myself, what was the Royal Air Force's loss would be the Army's gain. But the Royal Berkshire Regiment took a very similar view of the situation and I was amazed to find that I was equally unwanted in khaki.

'Go home and wait,' was the message, although a grizzled sergeant-major assured me, 'don't worry son, this war is going to last a long time'.

The chief petty officer who saw me when I tried to join the Royal Navy just laughed.

'Now what would we want with a racehorse trainer?' he wanted to know. 'Take a tip from me, sir. You try the Army. I believe the brown jobs still have some nags. The cavalry would suit you a treat.'

I left without a word. I could think of nothing to say. The sailor, of course, had been quite right. Fifty years earlier I would have been able to walk into the barracks of any hussar or lancer regiment. I would have been just the man to charge Fuzzy-Wuzzies in the desert or chase Boers across the veld. Wasn't I regarded as having one of the finest seats on a horse in the whole of England? Hadn't elegant ladies swooned throughout the length and breadth of France during the period when I lorded it as the dashing young manager of Lille's famous Croisè la Roche polo club. Didn't I know nearly everything there was to know about horses, having been brought up by one of the shrewdest judges of horseflesh in the world, my own father?

Sadly I had to confess to myself, as I drove home, that even if all my extravagant claims had been true there was no room for people like me in the present conflict. Mechanics and trained soldiers, that was what they needed. Men who had done a bit of soldiering, like the Territorials. Old men such as me were just a nuisance.

I can honestly say that I had never been more thoroughly down in the dumps in my life. Even the trim little stableyard at Sparsholt, which had been my pride and joy from 1933 up to the outbreak of war, had lost its charm. The horses, moving quietly in their boxes, seemed to emphasize my ostracism from a machine-mad world. For they were forbidden even to show themselves on a racecourse. The fear of providing targets for German bombers had led to the banning of racing, at least for the time being. It dawned on me that such a simple contribution as catering for the punters among the troops was barred to me and depressed me still further.

For me 1940 became a gloomy year indeed. Paris, where I had been born, was crushed beneath the German heel and France collapsed without allowing me to raise a hand in her defence. Nazi bombers dumped their loads on London and made their escape high over the Sussex downs where my father had spent his boyhood. I could not even be there to shake my fist at them. My father himself seemed to contribute more to the war effort. After spending the best part of his life in France he had returned home shrewdly in 1939 and, as the Battle of Britain developed, decided to take a hand. He bought himself an old bicycle for 10s., found himself lodgings, and at the age of 70 cycled to and from the Royal Armoured Corps depot at Didcot each day where he worked in an office throughout the war, boasting that never once was he late.

That was too much for me. Although I kept the horses in training for a time – I had about a dozen mixed flat racers and jumpers – just in case racing made a come-back, I decided to send them back to their owners. One by one the staff went too and in the end I shot the bolt on the last box and left myself. Despite further forays to various recruiting centres I was still rejected by the combatant services and therefore decided to follow in father's footsteps. By the end of 1940 I persuaded the relevant authorities that my experience of handling horseboxes made me an excellent potential heavy lorry driver – and got myself a job as a civilian employee at the R.A.F. depot in Milton, Gloucestershire. The fact that it was listed as a 'reserved occupation' I kept from my friends.

The next few months were certainly revealing. I learned for example why the R.A.F. stores were frequently short of nuts, bolts and spare parts. My colleagues, one of the toughest bunch of fellows I have ever met, regarded the huge articulated lorries we drove as a sort of travelling black market shop. They would stop their 'Queen Marys', as we called our vehicles, at garages all over East Anglia and the Midlands selling off stock. Considering that nearly all of them were ex-fairground hands, their ingenuity in fiddling their delivery notes and work sheets was masterly. Evidence of the profits they accrued was visible in the mammoth games of pontoon they played. It was nothing to see a swarthy Romany-type pull a roll of £400 from the top pocket of his greasy dungarees. I cannot say that I was popular with my fellow drivers. My refusal to help myself to what they regarded as a natural perk meant that no-one ever volunteered to accompany me as driver's mate. As one chap put it, he simply couldn't afford it. He had just privately disposed of a nice line in bicycles meant for guards patrolling the perimeter of airfields!

The management at Milton expressed surprise and concern when I announced in the late spring of 1941 that the army had at last condescended to accept me as a trooper in the Royal Armoured Corps. The gipsy drivers watched me go with obvious relief and got on with making their next million. My refusal to take part in their rackets had convinced them that I was dangerous. Volunteering for the army confirmed their suspicions that I was mad. Not long afterwards I had the feeling that perhaps they were right.

I can honestly say that I thoroughly enjoyed my first three weeks at Warminster depot, square-bashing and training to be a tank driver. Although I had no idea how tanks worked it seemed to come naturally to me to handle them and I roared gleefully over Salisbury Plain without a care in the world.

Once the initial period was finished, however, the routine of a training regiment set in. Scores of troopers who had completed their basic training hung about the camp while the powers-that-be tried to occupy their idle minds and hands by such brilliant schemes as ordering all boots to be greased thoroughly one day and when the grease had sunk well in, three days later, commanding that they should be blackened and polished again. The only bright spot I could discern on the horizon at this time was that I had been lucky enough to get a top bunk in the hut and thus avoided the nightly revels of my younger comrades, whose fondness for NAAFI beer being far from proportionate to their capacity, were frequently sick. Had I been in a bottom bunk life would have been unendurable instead of being merely uninteresting. Once again I found myself up against my age. The 18- and 19-year-olds in the camp regarded me as Methuselah and provided no companionship. The colonel, a decent old buffer, saw me as a potential ally and did his best to persuade me to become a driving instructor on the permanent staff, starting off as an acting, unpaid lance-corporal. He took a poor view of things when I was marched before him and declined.

'You don't know what you're missing, Goldsmith,' he said.

'No, sir! What am I missing?'

'Take this job and I'll guarantee you will be here safe and sound for the duration.'

That was the last thing I wanted and the thought of it threw me into despair. However, unknown to me, other forces were at work which were soon to remove me completely from the dubbin-and-drudgery brigade.

People became spies or secret agents in many ways, through their specialist knowledge and military training, tradition, a search for adventure and so on. I got into the business because my sister-in-law had to see her lawyer about arrangements connected with her divorce and remarriage. Normally an interview about such private matters as her's would have been conducted in the comfort of some discreet legal office but on this occasion the lawyer, John Chapman Walker, was recovering from a serious accident in which he had broken a number of bones. My sister-in-law insisted on finding out what sort of accident it had been, for she was a naturally curious woman. In the end he told her. The War Office had decided that with his legal training John was just the right type of person to interview potential agents. Unfortunately for him he ended up not only helping to select them but finding out just how dangerous some of their tasks were. Unlike many people in a similar position he thought it would be more correct to give advice if he had some experience in the job and so, while taking part in the agents' parachute course, he had come a cropper.

My sister-in-law was fascinated by this recital of his misfortune.

'I know just the man for your outfit,' she said. 'You ought to send for my brother-in-law. You won't be of much use to them any more, and he's just kicking his heels.'

She was quite right. At that moment I was making my lugubrious reappearance in the depot at Warminster, my mind blighted at the prospect of enduring the rest of the war teaching youngsters how to drive heaps of metal over the Downs.

A few days later a letter from my sister-in-law's husband, Captain Lionel Cecil, then serving in a crack cavalry regiment, lifted the gloom a little. I would, he wrote, be hearing soon about a job that I might find very interesting ... if I was accepted. With my previous experience of the age handicap, that apparently insurmountable barrier to a fuller life, I refused to let my hopes rise too far. Three weeks went by and I felt that my pessimism was probably justified. When my name appeared on orders, at the end of a list detailing fire pickets, guards and sanitary duty men, I was certain the end had come. I was to report to the colonel wearing my best battledress. This was it. He was going to insist on my becoming an instructor. My fate was to be linked for ever with the woes of Warminster.

It was an ominous confrontation. After I had been marched in 'Lef' ry', lef' ry', lef' ry' lef',' the old gentleman sat back and raised two pieces of paper, one in each hand.

Shaking them gently he stared at me and said: 'I've a letter and a warrant here for you, Goldsmith. You've to report to some place in London tomorrow. What is it all about?'

Quite truthfully I answered: 'I haven't a clue, sir.'

He eyed me suspiciously and then dismissed me. The orderly-room clerk fixed me up with a 48-hour pass and I departed joyfully for the guardroom and out through the main gate.

London came as a bit of a shock to me. After an interminable and uncomfortable train journey, jammed in a corridor with dozens of slumbering soldiers, I walked out of Paddington Station into the blacked-out streets, all wearing that peculiarly war-worn appearance. It was the first time I had been in London since 1939 and I hadn't realized how hard-hit it had been. The point was driven home more forcibly in the daylight, as I picked my way past bombed buildings and found the address to which I had to report.

It was a very ordinary-looking place, a large Victorian house, one of a number which had been commandeered by various ministries. There were not many people about and a clerk in army uniform asked me to wait. I took off my great-coat – it had been raining when I left camp – and hung it up with my beret. After a quarter of an hour the orderly reappeared and asked me to follow him. When I tried to put on my beret he told me not to waste time and I hurried after him. Somehow I felt that it was very unregimental to appear bare-headed.

The room I was shown into was practically bare of furniture. There were two chairs and a table behind which stood a thin man, of medium height, wearing a captain's insignia. Hatless and therefore unable to salute, I stood somewhat lamely to attention not having the slightest idea what I was doing there or what I was going to be asked to do.

The thin man, whose sharp features reminded me strongly of a weasel, told me to sit down.

'The whole idea is to see how good your French is,' he told me without wasting any time. 'From now on we will talk in French.'

So that was it. They were looking for interpreters. I might have known. Visions of a cushy number with the Free French Forces loomed up on the horizon.

After spending some time talking French, I was then asked

about French geography and customs. This puzzled me. What was the point of all these questions if I was only going to be an interpreter, I asked? My interrogator, having satisfied himself about my fluency, explained. I was regarded as a potential secret agent and would probably be dropped by parachute into France to carry out subversive work against the Germans. He added that although the department which would employ me would do all it could to help me beforehand, I would be on my own if I was caught.

Did I understand?

Of course I did, said I, and actually thought I did. I was unaware of the vast extent of my ignorance. I had simply no idea of the current situation in France, which I had not visited since 1938. I could imagine it only as it was then. If someone had mentioned the Gestapo to me at the very moment I was invited to become an agent, I honestly think that I would not have known what they were talking about.

A slightly more sombre note was introduced into the conversation by the interviewer telling me that, should I agree to go through with the training, I should tell my next of kin, i.e. my wife, and that she would be kept informed of my state of health while I was out of the country, by monthly letter. No one else was to be told any details of what had transpired.

'What about my C.O., sir?'

'Certainly not. It is most important that you should say nothing to anyone of what has been said in this room today. Now fall out, Goldsmith. You'll be hearing from us.'

I fell out, seized my beret and coat and left filled with elation. It looked as though I was going to get into the war at last.

Three weeks later Trooper Goldsmith's name again appeared on Orders at Warminster Camp. Once again I was marched before the commanding officer, very smart in my best battledress. He eyed me curiously.

'You've been posted,' he said. 'What is it all about?'

'I'm sorry, sir, I'm not quite sure,' I replied fairly truthfully. In fact, I had received a letter two days earlier saying that I would be leaving the Royal Armoured Corps training regiment and instructing me to report to an address in London.

'Ah, well, Goldsmith,' said my colonel. 'I'm sorry to lose you. I think you'll be sorry too one of these days. You would have had a great future here as an instructor on tracks (the army term for tank driving instructor) . . . been here for the duration. Still, there is no telling some people. Good luck to you, wherever you're going.'

'Thank you, sir.'

One step smartly back. Salute. Right turn. And exit Trooper Goldsmith to surrender side arms to armoury, hand in bedding and march clumsily down the road past the guardroom with a bulging kitbag slung on top of my pack, and sweltering in my greatcoat and equipment.

That night I slept in a little hotel in Paddington and dreamed that I was shoeing horses in the tank workshops. The following day I read for the umpteenth time the address given in my instructory letter and set off to find Orchard Court, a large block of flats in Portman Square.

Number 68 seemed innocent enough to me. I took a lift to the relevant floor, walked down a corridor and knocked at the number of the room I had been given. After a moment or two the features of the Weasel (I had by then learned that he was Selwyn Jepson, the well-known author) appeared round the door.

I saluted smartly, received a frown, and was ushered through a hall into a room on the right. There was no sign of anyone else.

Jepson wasted no time in spelling out what my immediate future would be. I would undergo different courses in sabotage, security, politics and parachute jumping. Plus a toughening-up course. If I got through all of them I would be considered ready for action in the field. If I didn't, some other job would be found for me or I might (horror of horrors) be returned to my unit. It all depended on me.

There was another thing. I would be given a temporary commission as a second-lieutenant.

'Now, go and buy yourself a couple of pips,' he said, 'and report here for duty in a week's time.'

I was shown out the way I had come in, still without seeing another soul.

It is a very pleasant experience to jump from trooper to officer in one morning and I thoroughly enjoyed clumping into a smart shop in Piccadilly and ordering my new badges of rank. Getting them sewn on was not so easy. The assistant, an elderly gentleman who was obviously used to dealing with more exalted ranks, did not share my mood of exuberance and took pleasure in saying that he could not arrange for them to be sewn on in the shop.

'Quite impossible, sir. Shortage of labour, you know.'

Considering there were two or three tailors and a few miles of thread in the establishment I thought this rather churlish, but refused to be put out. My next stop was the Hyde Park Hotel where I asked the attendant in the gentlemen's lavatory if he would do the job. A gnarled, old soldier, he was taken slightly aback, but thought he could find someone who would. If I would give him my battle-dress blouse. . . .

He disappeared and I took over the chair of the office in his cubby-hole. Within a quarter of an hour the attendant was back again with my newly-adorned jacket and I was able to relinquish my post. The five shillings I parted with nearly broke the bank but it was worth it.

I marched into the foyer and asked the girl at the switchboard if she would put through a personal call to my wife. The name, I said, was Goldsmith. While I waited by the desk I hummed to myself rather smugly. It would be a tremendous surprise for Tiny to learn that I had not only got the job I wanted but that I had also been commissioned.

'Your call, sir.'

I leaped to the phone but before I could say a word my wife, her voice full of excitement, said,

'Darling, isn't it wonderful. I'm so pleased you've got the job and been made an officer too.'

I was stunned. How on earth did she know.

'Don't be silly,' was her reply, 'the telephonist said Lieutenant Goldsmith was calling. It was obvious.'

I made a mental note to try to be as sharp-eyed as the telephonist!

The strange thing about my second visit to Orchard Court is the lack of impact it made on my memory. Perhaps it was because it was all so different from the first visit when I saw only Jepson. On this occasion there were many new faces about. There was Buckmaster, the head of the French section of the S.O.E., a tall thin man in army uniform. He made no strong impression on me except that his lips seemed to be constantly moist! André Simon, of the big French wine shippers, was also present, wearing R.A.F.

uniform. There may have been others but time has obliterated them from my memory. In any case, I was more struck by my fellow potential agents, to whom I was introduced for the first time. There were ten of us, all about to embark on the same training course. Apart from myself only one appeared to have had any military training, a shortish, broad-shouldered Captain with a thin black moustache which he fingered constantly. I gathered he had been brought back from the Middle East. The others were obviously unfamiliar with their uniforms, all of which were brand new and had strange creases and bulges which would have made the drill instructors at Warminster froth at the mouth.

A tall gangling French officer, at least six feet four inches tall, completed our little assembly and we were told that he would be our conducting officer during the course. Without much further ado we were dispatched to get on with the business of learning to be spies and the tall Frenchman, whom we later nicknamed Polydore, did his first bit of conducting by shepherding us into the back of an army lorry which set off at breakneck speed through the streets of London and finally into the countryside.

Polydore, having elected to travel in the driving cab as befitted his station, the rest of us were left to cling on to the lurching vehicle, making desultory conversation and trying to weigh each other up.

The boys in their new battledresses looked distinctly uncomfortable. As the journey progressed we fell silent, each man left alone with his thoughts. I looked round the faces. We had been told that our job, if we ever got into the field, would be dangerous. If we were caught we would be on our own. Which of us would have to go through that ordeal, I wondered? How many, if any, would die, and in what circumstances?

Fate had already made its selection. Although no one was aware of it, every mile the lorry covered through the leafy Hampshire lanes carried three of my companions nearer to death in the obscurity of concentration camps we had never even heard of at that time. For one man there was the added humiliation to face of dying in the knowledge that he had betrayed his own comrades.

Fortunately these things were hidden from us and the future held only the promise of excitement and adventure. Reality was a stranger.

3

I F it had not been for the stately homes of England I do not see
how we could possibly have got on with the war. As the years
went by and the island gradually became crowded with refugees,
dispossessed governments, alien soldiers and Americans, the
country's Georgian manors and Victorian 'seats' had to bear the
burden of housing the bloated army of administrators needed to
control the multitudes. Ministries, services and local authorities
fought for possession of aristocratic piles with a bitterness that
would have done credit to the combatants at Stalingrad. Just who
did the dirty work on behalf of S.O.E. I do not know, but they
certainly obtained their fair share of the nation's architectural
heritage and I, for one, was truly grateful. The months I spent in
training as a subversive agent were among the most enjoyable of
the war. It was a cross between going back to school and staying at
a series of first-class hotels where shooting, hunting and even
fishing were free.

My view of service life having been confined, up to then, to what
I could see from my top bunk at Warminster, I found the change
refreshing. If it had not been for the fact that the instruction given
on the various courses was aimed solely at teaching one to kill and
to destroy, it might even have been described as civilized.

The training was split into four parts. The first was a com-
mando-style military course, the second dealt with the political
and security aspects of subversion, the third with explosives and
sabotage and the fourth with parachute training.

The first stage of the induction of my own particular little squad
began when our lorry deposited us on the gravelled drive of Wan-
borough Manor in lovely rolling country near Guildford. A

charming, elderly major called de Wesselow welcomed us and we were shown to our quarters by a Jeeves-like orderly.

I was surprised to discover that our party of nine trainees, our conducting officer, the major, three giant sergeant instructors and a handful of general duty soldiers were the sole occupants of the manor. Each day began with a cross-country run on which we were accompanied by the indefatigable Major de Wesselow, who at the age of fifty kept himself fitter than many a younger man. After breakfast in a common mess, we would have lessons in map reading, or go down to the range for practice with Sten guns and Thompson sub-machine guns. Assault courses and physical endurance tests of a similar nature occupied the rest of our time. At night we repaired to the bar with our instructors and underwent further endurance tests designed to see how much alcohol we could consume without falling flat and also to see how we reacted while 'under the influence'. The Sergeants Three, who seemed to be impervious to any quantity of liquor, had a nasty habit of ordering a round of pints about 10 p.m. and then, just as we were downing them, announcing: 'Well gentlemen, we've got a nice little scheme for you. Rendezvous at the main gate in a quarter of an hour in battle order and we will see just how good you are at making your way across strange country at night.'

They were remarkable men, indifferent to the weather and, in fairness to them, they never asked anyone to do anything that they could not do themselves.

The basic training, with its healthy outdoor emphasis, suited me down to the ground and, as far as I could gather, most of my companions. I was sorry when our three weeks' preliminary training was over and we were all sent on seven days' leave.

While we relaxed at home the confidential reports submitted by our instructors and the conducting officer were thoroughly scrutinized by our masters and when I reported back to Orchard Court I noticed that three of our original party were missing. Their absence was unexplained.

That left six of us. There was Amps, a stocky, ruddy-cheeked little man who claimed he had been a jockey in France and who looked, dressed and behaved like a stable lad. His French was good but he did not have much of a clue when it came to paper work and codes. He made a special friend of Staggs, another bantam, with a sallow face and a thin, black pencil moustache. Staggs, I believe, had been in business in France before the war.

John Young, a couple of years my junior, was married to a French girl he had met while travelling for an insurance company. He spoke fractured French with a strong Newcastle accent. I did what I could to help him improve it but without success. As the weeks passed I could sense him losing confidence, but he stubbornly refused to give up, his blue eyes staring defiantly from under a mop of black hair. Conversely Gilbert Norman, a fully-fledged captain and a superb athlete, was absolutely bursting with self-assurance. Whatever we did in physical training he could always do that little bit better. His French was excellent.

The final member of our party was a young French student, about twenty-two years old, whom we christened 'Science-Po' because he never stopped talking about his intention to study political science ('Science Politique') after the war. He seemed nervous and out of place. He was also frightened of Polydore.

Polydore was becoming a nuisance. He talked incessantly, knew better than everyone and criticized everything. What little confidence we had had in him evaporated when we started our political and security course at Beaulieu, where S.O.E. had a number of houses on the fringes of the New Forest. It became obvious that Polydore, despite his talk, had never been 'in the field'.

Beaulieu contained an unpleasant surprise for the more naïve of us – including myself. It was here that the news was broken to us about just how rough and tough the Gestapo were likely to be. Our instructors, pukka officers in the Intelligence Corps, had no personal experience, but they had gathered some impressive and frightening information which left us in no doubt about what to expect. This grim knowledge injected a more serious tone into our studies. Partly these consisted of a good deal of play-acting, learning how to behave naturally in the most unnatural circumstances. For example how to react if, say, you were in a café in France waiting to meet someone when suddenly the Gestapo walked in. It would be no good dropping your coffee cup with a clatter, or choking over a mouthful of food. Nor could one get away by ostentatiously whistling a merry tune and strolling out without paying the bill.

26

To be prepared for such a situation may sound elementary, but it was vital for an agent to become a good actor if he did not wish to end up playing the leading role in a tragedy ending with a death-bed scene. Innocent people do not jump when suddenly confronted with the presence of the local police forces – spies do – unless they have been equipped with a dead-pan face. This the Beaulieu experts did their best to provide. If they found a receptive pupil in me it was solely due to my misspent youth. Had all their students been the sons of horse dealers I am sure they would have achieved 100 per cent success with this part of the curriculum.

As a boy it was my duty to demonstrate the virtues of my father's nags for the benefit of prospective customers. Whatever the visitor wanted – a hack, a hunter, steeplechaser or officer's charger – he was likely to be offered the same horse. Father obtained these all-purpose animals from the slaughter-house at Vaugirard.

Once in our yard the poor devil's feet would be seen to and a set of shoes fitted. Then father would clip him out, applying the chain-driven clippers vigorously while I turned a handle like mad to keep them going. We did not have electric clipping machines in those days. The coat having been clipped out, the animal would be turned over to me for grooming with a wisp of twisted hay and a small bottle of petrol. After an hour and a half my arms would be aching but the horse would be transformed. His coat would wear a silk-like sheen and he would be given pride of place in a box fine enough to house a Derby winner.

The result was that when the unsuspecting buyer explained his needs my father was in a position to say he had 'just the animal', a splendid creature, and 'I'll put the boy up to put him through his paces.' Out would come the refugee from the slaughter-house and if he had to jump then I made him jump. If he had any strange little habits, like shying at passers-by, I restrained him. Applying my heel and leg always on the blind side away from the viewer, I literally held the beast together.

And when my father made extravagant claims on the horse's behalf I made sure my features conveyed only genuine respect for the creature. To look a man straight in the eye and tell him a lie requires years of practice; to show no reaction at all to given situations demands a little longer. I was fortunate enough to have a start over most of my colleagues at Beaulieu.

On more than one occasion in the years to come the facial control I learned on the back of an animal plucked from the gates of the abattoirs at Vaugirard saved me from ending up in a different sort of slaughter-house.

At Beaulieu, other techniques were imparted on the do's and don'ts of being an agent, such as how to make sure that you were not being followed – or that you were. Codes and ciphers were studied. Where to stay and how to pass on messages, when to move from one address to another and what to say if casually questioned at a street control, everything that could possibly be learned and practised in theory was drummed into us.

Perhaps the most important thing we learned was to rely on ourselves for our own security. There was no golden rule book. You made your own rules. Just like the Germans.

At the end of the course at Beaulieu I was sent out on a scheme to see just how much I had learned. My instructions were to travel to Leeds with certain documents, meet another agent in a café and hand them over. Other agents, in the meantime, would try to pick me up, acting the role of Gestapo officers.

I must have proved most annoying to my interrogators when eventually I was captured. To start with they couldn't find any documents. And secondly they were mortified to hear that I had spotted the man they sent to tail me almost immediately and had spent a considerable time tailing him. This was not particularly clever of me but due more to the distinctive physical characteristics of the man on my trail. A lot of Americans walk in an extraordinary manner, upright in the back, but bent at the knee and bent at the elbow, as if they were carrying a small Stars and Stripes in each hand while they stepped over a series of small obstacles. Furthermore, their trousers are frequently pulled up an inch too high as if they are intent on gelding themselves and at the same time cooling their ankles. This applies especially to big Americans and I reckon that the one I saw hanging about near the hotel I booked into was one of the biggest. His name was John Tyson and he had been sent over by the United States equivalent of S.O.E., that now familiar organization the O.S.S., to study our methods. He began to wear his trousers an inch lower the day after

I spotted him and we have remained the best of friends to this day.

To return to the 'secret' papers, they are probably where I put them to this day if the café still exists. Deciding they were too hot to have in my pocket all the time, I bought a yellow oilskin tobacco pouch, wrapped them in it, sealed it with tape and hid it in the cistern of the gents. Without this as evidence my 'captors' found it very difficult to pin anything on me.

Lack of incriminating evidence was a legal nicety the real Gestapo chose to ignore when they actually did arrest me, but it is interesting to note also that they too neglected to search the lavatory cistern of the café in which I was seized, or anywhere else come to that, although I might have hidden all sorts of fascinating documents on the premises. All of which goes to show that the renowned German thoroughness did not always apply.

That our own security and intelligence training could have been better early in 1942 there is no doubt, but one has to remember that S.O.E. was a make-shift organization which did not come into being until after the fall of France and that, apart from returning escapers and reports from the very small number of agents in Europe, there was very little to go on at that time. One had to experience life in Occupied Europe to be able to assess it. As time went on, our training systems put into practice the lessons learned from men in the field. The Germans no doubt did the same.

After three weeks at Beaulieu came another seven days' leave period, spent quietly with my second wife whom I married at the end of 1940; my first marriage had ended in divorce. I was thankful that I was no longer a bachelor. For some agents a happy marriage and a good wife were undoubtedly valuable stabilizing factors and positive assets while on active service. Agents with unhappy marriages were at a definite disadvantage, as I was to have tragically revealed to me.

Once our leave was over all six of us joined Polydore, whose constantly patronizing air had become even more odious, to be led off inevitably to another country house, this time on the wild and beautiful coast of Inverness. There, in the lovely countryside around Arisaig, we played deadly forms of Boy Scout games which included sneaking up silently behind the senior officer, a tough major from a Scottish regiment, who always wore the kilt. If you got close enough to touch it without him hearing you, then you could consider you were a safe bet to polish off a German sentry without a peep coming out of him. If Major Watts did hear you coming, you were in trouble.

Perhaps I was lucky, but the weather seemed to be very pleasant during our stay in Arisaig and the training, unarmed combat, fieldcraft, weapon training and demolition work, was enjoyable. At least most of it was. The handling of P.E., the plastic explosive used extensively for subversive work, had one unpleasant side-effect. It could be moulded into any shape and size and was quite safe, refusing to explode even when thrown or even hit by a bullet. But the nasty almond paste smell was oppressive. And as all charges for an operation were normally prepared indoors beforehand, it was quite common for men handling them for long periods in a smallish room to finish up with a splitting headache sometimes bad enough to affect their competence. As far as I know this problem was not overcome, although I never heard that it interfered with actual sabotage. P.E. was set off by thrusting pencil detonators well into the yellow plastic mass. Reliable from the point of view that they nearly always functioned, I never knew a single one of these detonators to go off on time, a weakness I took pains to impress on Resistance fighters when later I had to instruct them in France.

Poaching was also among the lessons taught at Arisaig, but most people preferred obtaining their salmon with the assistance of a small charge of P.E. This was something that could be indulged in during boating instruction although I preferred to spend this time in the well-stocked saloon of a yacht lent by a local tycoon, swapping racing yarns over his gin.

I think everyone was sorry when we eventually left Arisaig for Ringway, via Orchard Court, to do our parachute jumps. 'Science Po' did not go with us. I gathered that he had drawn the line at parachuting.

He was not the only one. On the first day of the course, while we were practising in the gymnasium, I asked Polydore if he had ever jumped before. He replied that he hadn't and that he wasn't going to.

'Oh, yes you bloody well are,' I replied. 'If you don't you are going back wherever you came from.' Conducting officers were supposed to do everything their squad did and Polydore knew this.

'Well,' I asked him, 'do you or don't you jump?'

'I don't,' he said.

That night Gilbert Norman, being the senior officer, got on the phone to Orchard Court. The following day Polydore packed his bags and left us without a word. He had been recalled to explain himself and we never saw him again. Now there were five . . .

That morning Staggs and Amps who had never been up in a plane before were given a joy ride just to give them some idea and later we all piled into a lorry to see a battalion of the Parachute Regiment giving an exhibition. We left our billet in the best of humour, singing at the tops of our voices.

We returned silent and crestfallen. One of the paratrooper's 'chutes had roman-candled – failed to open – and he had plunged into the ground only fifty yards from where we were standing. We remained rooted to the spot, rigid with horror, while Parachute Regiment officers hurried over and ascertained that the man was dead. They made no attempt to remove the body and as one of them went past I asked: 'You aren't going to leave him there, are you?'

'Got to, old boy,' was the reply. 'Must let the experts have a look at the 'chute and find out what happened. We don't want it to happen to anyone else do we?'

Gloomy silence descended over our company. We were all greatly relieved when the practice jumps went without a hitch – just as I think we were all rather astonished to realize that the course was over and we were ready to go into action – that we were now agents.

4

I LANDED IN France frightened, furious, swearing and soaked to
the skin. It was not what I had intended. The scene of my in-
glorious arrival was the Riviera and I doubt whether any of the
smart set who had known me during my period as a polo club
manager would have condescended to recognize me. Yet I had
only myself to blame.

After my training had finished at the end of June, the course
was split up. Gilbert Norman and Staggs disappeared to receive
further instruction as radio operators, Amps went off somewhere
else and John Young and I repaired to an hotel in Kensington
where S.O.E. had a whole floor for the use of agents. There our
wives joined us. John, it turned out, was also destined for further
training – as a radio operator, and I was glad for his sake because
it meant that his terrible French accent would not be such a
dangerous handicap.

As for myself, I was prepared for operations in the near
future. My mission was to set up a small sabotage circuit in the
Abbeville-Amiens area after finding and training my own recruits.
This was a tough nut to crack as the towns lay in a zone where the
Germans were particularly numerous and active and I discussed
the problems with Buckmaster at Orchard Court. I suggested
that it would be much better if I got myself acclimatized first
in the Unoccupied Zone, the *Zone Libre*, before sticking my
neck out. There was so much to pick up since my last visit to
France in 1938 – to the races. There were facts about politics;
what it was practical to ask for in the shops; who the latest film
stars and what the songs of the moment were? Not to know
these everyday things could sometimes make one much more con-

spicuous than a major blunder, such as a badly forged document.

In the South of France, although there were plenty of German agents about, and Italians too, the pressure was not so great. Furthermore there was much talk of a strong Resistance organization there which I might be able to contact and report back on to London. The vision of the secret army was already fixed in the minds of the controllers of S.O.E. What they needed was proof that the information they had received about its numbers, its leaders and its weapons was true. By sending me in through the Riviera, the big chiefs in London might pick up a small bonus in the way of corroboration of details already in their hands. Buckmaster had another reason to be pleased with my suggestion. Only a limited number of planes were available for infiltrating agents and the Riviera run was made by boat.

Visits to Orchard Court followed almost daily after my task had been allotted. The form they took may have been necessary but at the time they struck me as being farcical and I have learned nothing since to change my opinion. I refer to the practice of sticking visiting agents in different rooms and the growth of what may now be called The Black Bathroom Syndrome. In theory it was a sound idea that when a man went to Orchard Court, or any other 'jumping off' headquarters for that matter, he should not see, or be seen by, other agents. This eliminated the possibility of someone starting suddenly when confronted by a familiar face in unfamiliar surroundings – such as the local Gestapo offices. In order to achieve this end, an agent who called at No. 68 was generally hustled into one or other of the rooms there so as to leave the corridors empty. If a larger number of callers than usual had arrived it was even possible to find oneself thrust into the bathroom which was decorated with black tiles.

As required, you would be called from your hiding place and ushered into the presence of whoever demanded it. As the door opened for your departure from your superior anyone in the corridors would make themselves scarce and that was that. Secrecy had been preserved – until the evening, or perhaps lunchtime. For although S.O.E. had taken every precaution to shield their protégés while inside the building they did nothing to prevent a glaring lack of security outside it. Anyone who wished to find a comrade he had trained with, or whom he had met 'in the field' –

the term used for an agent on active service overseas – had only to go to the bar of the Gay Nineties in Berkeley Street. You could see as many as six in the bar at one time on occasions, with their wives or their girl-friends. Of course, you were not supposed to know who they were. And they did not let on that they knew who you were. But with chance meetings on courses, or on missions, it was only natural that an awful lot of people got to know each other. When you consider that the men had all been trained to be observant and spot their own kind, it was not surprising. There is only one consolation to be found. The Germans were so obsessed with the importance of getting a man into Orchard Court they missed a great opportunity to strike at a much better place. If they could have placed a spy behind the bar at the Gay Nineties he could have helped to shop the lot of us.

Much more impressive than the security arrangements was the equipment department. According to my cover story I was to take on the character of a spiv called Jean Delannoy. I chose the name myself; Delannoy was a leading French film director and I felt sure I would not forget it. I pushed up my age by a few years to make sure that I was not hauled in under the *service obligatoire* regulations and forced to go to work in Germany or on war installations in Occupied France.

If questioned about my antecedents I would tell my own life story up to the time I left France in 1933. After that I would spin out a story fitting in real episodes and places wherever possible. I was solemnly warned that this 'cover story' was to be the touchstone to guide me through my career. If captured I was to stick to it and on no account was I to deviate or try any other method of talking myself out of a jam. I listened and promised to obey.

I was taken to the tailor and told to choose a cloth for my suit in keeping with my role as a black-market dealer. The pad of samples he produced was a masterpiece. All the cloth was from patterns currently being worn in France and the suit he produced was of the correct, hideous style, then in vogue among spivs. Shoes, socks and other garments I bought for myself with cash supplied by the ungrudging cashiers at S.O.E., making sure that they were the right pattern. I emerged from this sartorial exercise as nattily dressed a foreign wideboy as you can imagine, much to the disgust of my wife, who had to endure it whenever we went out. All agents were sensibly required to wear their 'issue' for some time before they set out in order to give them a suitably shabby appearance. New suits stuck out like sore thumbs in a country where, by 1942, cloth was a rare commodity. Only my shoes were allowed to retain a brilliant gleam. Polish was on the black market in France and, as a dealer, I could be expected to have access to supplies.

Towards the end of September I was given a British passport to add to my false papers. In it I was described as a civil servant in order to give me the necessary status should the plane which was to carry me to Gibraltar, en route for the Riviera, be forced to land in Spain.

Two fairly useless items had also been delivered. One was a phial of poison which was sewn under the lapel of my gent's natty suiting for use if the Gestapo proved to be better runners than I. My objections to this were two-fold. First it was, I felt, bad for morale. Secondly, it was a certain give-away if anyone did fall into the hands of the enemy. Once the Gestapo had discovered it they were hardly likely to accept the explanation that I had bought it on the black market, nor were they likely to give agents the opportunity of swallowing the poison once it was found. I resolved to throw it away at the first opportunity, in case I was ever stupid enough to consider using it.

Useless item Number Two was my code name – Valentin. By this alone I was to be known while on active service. Code names subsequently became a pet aversion of mine. Although I had been born and bred in France I had never heard of anyone who was actually called Valentin. It might have been an excellent way of identifying an agent in messages to London but, in the field, it could possibly be dangerous. Code names became ever more ludicrous as time went on; had people actually used some of these names they would have given themselves away in no time. I met one girl, of whom more later, who sported the incredible name of Binette – the French word for a garden hoe. For my part I used my code name only in very special circumstances. I remained what I had been all of my life, Jean – French pronunciation, of course.

5

M Y final departure for the scene of operations was un-
dramatic. Having assured himself that I had left no
London bus tickets in my pockets and that there were no English
labels on my clothes, my conducting officer wished me luck and
sent me home for the evening. The next morning I kissed my wife
goodbye at our Kensington hotel, entered the car which 'the office'
had sent for me, and drove to Waterloo. My wife spoiled this aus-
tere farewell by reappearing at the station with some trifle she
thought I had left behind and might need. She said later that she
waved until the train had disappeared from sight.

Portsmouth was my first stop. There I joined a motley collection of servicemen and uncommunicative civilian passengers.
Most of them fell asleep and as the plane flew through the night I
wondered how many of those aboard were described in their pass-
ports as 'civil servants' like myself. I was no wiser when we
touched down at Gibraltar.

Here I was to pick up a felucca which would take me to Cannes.
A felucca is a small, slow Mediterranean trading boat of about
twenty tons which must be unpleasant to travel in at the best of
times. In the hands of an eccentric Polish naval officer and a pirati-
cal one-man crew it quickly takes on an almost vicious character.
During a storm it becomes homicidal.

We left Gibraltar in almost perfect weather, chugging slowly out
into the night watching the lights of Algeciras dancing across the
waters to where the dark bulk of The Rock blotted out our view of
the stars. The air was warm and pleasant. With three other passengers bound for the same place, I sat on a hatch cover and relaxed. I
have never been particularly fond of the sea, probably because I

swim only three strokes before sinking like a stone, but this trip appeared to have the aura of a pleasant cruise. A brilliant white flash in the middle of a black beard showed that our skipper was also pleased with life.

My fellow travellers on this trip were Sidney Jones, code-name Felix, later to be betrayed to the Gestapo and executed: F. Chalmers Wright, of the Political Warfare Executive, and a small, fat Frenchman who was back in Britain in less than three months with an improbable tale about conducting a running fight down a railway line with the Germans and escaping over the Pyrenees.

With these companions the next two days passed uneventfully, apart from the inconvenience of having to skulk below deck whenever other ships hove into sight. Gradually, however, the drawbacks of felucca travel began to make themselves felt, in particular the primitive sanitary arrangements or, more correctly, the complete absence of them.

Squatting over the gunwale of the low-lying felucca you could reflect on the simple comforts you take for granted at home, especially when the sea slapped coldly against an exposed bottom. Slowly our clothes became saturated with sea water and Sidney Jones remarked that they would be a dead give-away if we were to be picked up soon after landing. The prospect of ever setting foot on dry land again began to recede on the third night, however, as a fresh breeze became a howling wind and driving rain and foam lashed the boat. Huddled below, unable to see what was going on but able to hear the thudding of the waves and the wind shrieking in the rigging. I was too scared to be ill. The little boat pitched crazily, sometimes standing on her head, sometimes on her tail. For three days we bucketed on through the gale. On the fourth it became too much even for our redoubtable Pole.

Staring wildly at our pale faces he announced with a big smile, 'Ve are going to seenk. Ze storm, she weel seenk us.' Personally I looked forward to the release but some stronger spirit demanded to know if there was anything we could do to help.

The Pole flashed his madman's smile again and shrugged his shoulders.

'Nothings to do,' he said. 'You stay here.' And with that he vanished up the stairs again. Sidney Jones nobly followed him, took one look at the sea and came back.

'He's right, you know,' he said. 'We'll just have to sit here.' And sit we did for another thirty-six hours while the gale played itself out. During this period our Polish skipper appeared once more in our midst, beaming and holding out the little finger of his right hand. He had cut it on a tin of beans (the storm had not affected his appetite) and it had turned septic.

'Pliz, you cut it off?' he asked the little Frenchman who responded with a low moan and shut his eyes in horror at the thought. 'Pliz, you cut it for me?' the assembled company was asked *en masse*.

We looked at him wanly and shook our heads as one man. He gave another shrug of his massive shoulders and disappeared obviously puzzled at our squeamishness. I think even his own crewman, a tough customer if ever I saw one, declined to perform the operation for the skipper still had his finger, crudely bandaged, when last I saw him.

The trip took nine days in all and I can say in all honesty that they were the worst nine days I experienced during the war. By the time we reached Cannes I think that not one of our little party would have accepted £1,000 to spend another day on that foul-smelling, cramped, filthy little boat.

No stable I have ever seen smelled worse than that felucca, and how Sidney Jones, who worked for Elizabeth Arden before the war, endured it so stoically is a mystery to me. And yet it looked at one time as though we might have to face the prospect of spending still longer aboard once we had arrived off Cannes, for there was no answer to our signal. We gave the pre-arranged light flashes but received no response from the coast. Had the reception committee given up waiting for us because of the delay caused by the storm? Had they been picked up by the police? The only way to find out was to go and see. It would have been possible to call off the operation and return to Gibraltar if we had any real suspicion that all was not well but the thought of another sea drama wiped that out of our minds. We decided to take the felucca as close inshore as was practical and then one of us would take a small rubber dinghy and paddle ashore to spy out the land. If the reception committee were waiting, the boat could be called in.

As I had no address to go to whether the committee were there or not, I volunteered for the job, inspired mainly by my desire to escape from my loathsome surroundings. I lowered myself into the bobbing dinghy which the Polish able seaman had made ready. He gave me a push, I gave the felucca a firm dig in the ribs with my paddle, and I was off.

The shore looked much farther away from the seat of the dinghy than it did from the deck of the felucca. It was forbidding and mysterious. Steadily, in the best Arisaig manner, I pulled towards the beach hoping that I was not being watched by some pro-German coastguard or Vichy policeman. For although this was supposed to be the Unoccupied Zone any agent picked up was likely to be handed over to the Gestapo who were operating throughout the area in large numbers.

As I drew nearer, the dark mass of the dunes split up and I could distinguish tufts of coarse grass and low bushes. Finally I could see shadowy figures near a small tree. The dinghy was gliding smoothly into the beach and I hoisted myself over the side. Any moment now I would know whether the reception committee was genuine or false. 'Well, here goes,' I said to myself, and stepped out straight into six feet of water. Gasping, spluttering, completely immersed I struck out wildly. I had completely forgotten that on this stretch of coast the beach shelves steeply (this was the reason for using feluccas which can come close in to the shore). Fortunately for me two or three desperate strokes enabled me to ground in the shallows on my knees and stagger ashore like a drowned rat. The reception committee looked on amazed, shushing me in alarm at the noise I was making.

The dinghy which I should have buried carefully in the sand I dispatched seawards with a vicious kick and it floated forlornly away. As I did so muffled figures grasped me by the arms and helped me ashore.

'We were expecting four men,' one of them said. 'Which one are you.'

'Valentin,' I spat out ungraciously. 'And a bloody wet Valentin at that.'

Once I had convinced them of my authenticity my only concern was to get the felucca inshore as quickly as possible and make my way to some place where I could get into dry clothes. Once the correct signal had been given the little vessel puttered in to the beach, a gangplank was run out and my companions landed dry shod, staring curiously at my dripping figure. No time was wasted, however, and as soon as our suitcases had been unloaded and spirited away by one of the reception committee, some hapless traveller boarded the felucca for the journey back to Gibraltar, the Pole flashed his dazzling smile and the boat put out to sea again.

Some time later I heard that our Polish friend had shot himself dead while playing Russian roulette with a compatriot in Gibraltar. I was not surprised.

The reception committee from Carte* was much larger than I had expected and there was a certain amount of noise and confusion; but eventually the party split up and I squelched my way after a total stranger into the darkness. Sidney Jones, dapper as ever, came with me. Within fifteen minutes we were crunching up the gravel path of a garden, with tall pines swaying gently overhead and the leaves of mimosa trees rustling in the slight breeze. A bird-like little man with bright eyes and a pink face helped me out of my clothes when we had entered the small kitchen. André Bartoli, the owner of the villa was one of the right-hand-men of Carte and fortunately for me, one of the most discreet. He put me in a chair in his kitchen where I sat in one of his dressing-gowns feeling anything but the intrepid saboteur I was supposed to be. André, head of a considerable insurance firm, did his best not to laugh at the sight of my long lean body draped in his minute robe.

My stay at the Villa Caracasa was brief. The next day I made my way to another villa, owned this time by a broad-shouldered Corsican, Paulo Leonetti. Monsieur Leonetti, who was then in his early fifties, was a dedicated opponent of the Nazis and of the Vichy government. A former mayor of Antibes, a couple of miles or so up the coast, he had been approached after the Armistice in 1940 and asked to be more co-operative. When he indicated that he preferred to hold his own views he was badly beaten up by the Vichy police. The beating merely confirmed his opinion of the New Order.

Anyone who knew Leonetti could have told his persecutors they were wasting their time. Coming to the Côte d'Azur from

* The code-name of André Girard and the resistance organization he set up. An account of its inception is given on pp. 43–44.

Bastia, before the First World War, he had served as an N.C.O. in the 141st Regiment of Infantry, a Marseilles formation, until his capture at Verdun in 1917. He was fond of telling the story of his attempted escape when he lowered a rope from a fortress window with a cooking pot on the end to hang like a plumb-line. All would have gone well had not one of three Irish soldiers who were making the attempt with him put his foot through a window on the way down. The Germans hadn't been so gentle with him on that occasion and he had not forgotten. Now when anything was needed in the area by the embryo Resistance forces the old soldier was always the first man called in. 'Leonetti, we want this.' 'Leonetti, we want that.' It was always Leonetti. As the local hairdresser, Leonetti was able to be in contact with a lot of people without arousing suspicion. At the same time when he took me in he knew that he was risking not only his life but those of his wife and three children as well. To me his sturdy figure, with a black Basque beret neatly covering his well-groomed hair, is an unforgettable picture. He exemplified the spirit of the Resistance long before it became popular, when liberation seemed very far away.

Having arrived and settled in I now had to get down to work, and very pleasant it proved to be to start with. My first job was to blend with the countryside – that is I had to superimpose a Riviera tan on my conspicuous white skin. Early each morning I would slip away from the house and find a deserted spot on the beach to sunbathe. To complete the picture I wore a pair of young Paulo Leonetti's trousers rolled up to just below the knee as was the fashion in those days. While I lay there I did a fair amount of thinking. I decided that on no account could anyone in the Carte organization know that I was a British officer or even that I was English until I knew a great deal more about their set-up. As an added security measure I confined my trips to and from Leonetti's to the early morning or late evening and resolved to discover other houses which I could use at irregular intervals. My aim was to give the locals the impression that I was a young Parisian who had come to the south of France to avoid compulsory service under the Germans in the Occupied Zone. In that way I could be sure of the sympathy of most people, for every Frenchman prefers to work for himself. Information about people in the area I built up gradually from talks with Leonetti, particularly after his visits to the local brothel where he did the girls' hair. These visits were rewarded with a bowl of highly-spiced tomato sauce prepared by the madame in appreciation of the fact that he gave his regular-customers cut rates. Sometimes I was able to add to the rations a variety of small fish called *rascasse* which Paulo and I brought back from brief fishing trips, during which we kept well within the 100 yard limit imposed by the coastal authorities. The sea air helped my tan.

Mobility was my next obstacle. A car was out of the question and public transport between the small villages and towns I would have to visit was either non-existent or too dangerous. There was nothing for it but a bicycle. Paulo found a magnificent machine in a shop in Nice and we went down to inspect it together. Never before or since have I seen such a beauty. It was made entirely of aluminium and had drop handlebars. I could not wait to return to Leonetti's and arrange its purchase. This took some time. Orchard Court had issued me with brand-new notes, mainly, I gathered, on the grounds that many more could be carried. Given the fact that hard cash was one of the things that was always in demand throughout the war; new currency had its drawbacks. Any agent masquerading as a working man would find great difficulty in explaining how he came to be carrying a fortune in new notes. I even heard of two agents who were picked up because, although they denied knowing each other, they had equal amounts of unused notes which bore consecutive serial numbers. One man's bank roll began where the other's ended! I believe Buckmaster blamed agents in Lisbon for having supplied the notes on that occasion, but mine certainly came from London. Paulo and I spent some time rubbing grime into the notes I had brought with me and Père Leonetti gave me some from his shop, tucking the London notes away to be disbursed cautiously in the months ahead.

Once the bicycle had been purchased and I had achieved suntanned anonymity, I felt that I could put the next stage of my plans into operation and establish a trial sabotage school on which I could model things when I finally went north. Carefully I selected houses and flats where I could stay the night safely while away from Leonetti's and after that, with the aid of Bartoli, with whom I was becoming more and more friendly, 'Classrooms' in Cannes,

Antibes and Nice. The one in Nice was a flat just opposite the police station. A small band of pupils was carefully vetted and all was ready for Goldsmith to pass on the teachings he had absorbed at Arisaig.

Over a period of days I unpacked the contents of my precious suitcase. One by one I dismantled the three Sten guns it contained and wrapped them in my jacket which I carried strapped to the pannier of my aluminium racer. I had started out with the idea that I might transport the parts under potatoes in the pannier. Then someone pointed out that if any gendarme saw me with a load of food in ration-conscious France he was almost certain to stop me and question me as to whether I had obtained it on the black market. These wise words having been absorbed and acted on I distributed my weapons and later the explosives and detonators between the three sabotage schools. At last I was in business.

Night after night in the blacked-out flats, solemn shopkeepers, clumsy peasants and deft mechanics would learn how not to put their fingers in the ejection aperture of the Sten, how to mould plastic explosive and where to stick the time pencils. A few of them went away with headaches from handling the P.E. in the confined space, but by obeying strict security regulations they came to no further harm. This passion for security increased as I had more opportunities to see the Carte organization at work. My criticism was all the more pointed because had the circuit been properly run there should have been nothing for me to see.

The origins of Carte and its subsequent development are interesting because they are woven through the network of all my experiences in France during the war. Carte came into being almost automatically after the blitzkrieg had brought France to a humiliating armistice table. Although possibly the majority of the people were glad of the respite, were content to wait and see how Hitler's New Order in Europe would develop, there were still plenty of dissidents who, from the very beginning of Nazi domination, were determined to fight back.

The Riviera, in the Unoccupied Zone, gave more scope to the rebels than most areas. The coast line was one of its principal assets. The bays, the small towns, the long deserted beaches with deep water just off shore, made the landing of illegal passengers and cargo reasonably simple. Today the coastal roads and the resorts have been developed to the point where it is hard to believe that this was ever a quiet coast. Beaches which now are overlooked by towering hotels were deserted in 1940. Many of the inhabitants of the small towns were experienced sailors or professional fishermen, an advantage for potential Resistance groups. The population as a whole was used to dealing with foreign visitors, was more cosmopolitan than in inland towns, and contained many artists and other bohemians. All along the coast small groups of men met to discuss the best ways to fight back. Old soldiers were called upon. Businessmen became involved. As early as July 1940 the seeds were sown. Among the first to plant them was André Girard.

Girard was an artist, and a man of immense charm. He was also a patriot who burned with a genuine passion to see his country free. He was soon in contact with the numerous embryo groups along the Côte d'Azur and took for himself the code name of Carte. About 41 at the time, he was bursting with ideas. The trouble was that they followed so closely on the heels of each other that nothing ever came of them. But his fame spread and with it his contacts until in the end he was known by, and knew of, groups which stretched well into the domain of Occupied France. In his studio in Antibes he gave the impression that he had but to give the signal and thousands of men would rise to arms. Better still, he claimed to have, and undoubtedly did have, connections in the Vichy army who had promised their support. Little wonder that London thought he was the answer to their prayers.

At that time, no one had really grasped how the secret army everyone dreamed of was going to be constructed. Girard seemed to offer a solution. Although the supply of arms was going to be a problem, for Britain needed everything she could produce to defend herself against invasion, at least there was evidence of a will to resist on a large scale.

All sorts of people were handled by Carte reception committees during 1942 and the beginning of 1943. A Belgian cabinet minister, senior French officers and various others went out. Important British agents came in, among them Bodington, one of the staff chiefs at Orchard Court. Not everyone came and went quietly. General Bloch D'Assaut, the eminent armoured warfare expert reached the coast but refused to board an outgoing submarine. Solemnly he told Bartoli: 'Pierre (that was his code name), I am a French general, and a French general dies in France.' Whereupon the iron man returned to Paris where he proved to be ten times more efficient than his melodramatic pronouncement might have suggested, becoming a positive pain in the neck to the Germans. Yet another dignitary reached the environs of Cannes but refused to board the incoming submarine unless his secretary could travel with him. The harassed reception committee immediately contacted London and received clearance for the secretary, only to be told at this point that she would not leave without two of her close relations. This time the reception committee put their foot down and the secretary sailed with her boss and left her family behind.

Procrastination was probably the deadliest enemy of all who had to use clandestine methods of entering and leaving France. Big Wigs and Brass Hats did not seem to realize that by standing on ceremony they were putting the lives of women and children in danger. André Bartoli's villa was in constant use despite the fact that his wife and three children were in residence. It took him all his time to enforce his rule that only one guest should dine with the family at a time.

More often than not, two complete strangers would find themselves sitting at the ancient table in the dining-room, gazing sleepily at the woodworm holes and admiring, perhaps, the sturdy Louis Seize writing desk. For many the visit to the Villa Caracasa meant a brief and pleasant evening to be remembered during long nights of excitement, noise, terror and even death. The ghosts of brave men haunt the shadows of the garden that leads towards the sea.

It was during one of my solitary visits to the Bartoli residence that I was told I would meet the legendary Raoul, a name I had heard quite often before leaving London. Raoul was the S.O.E. code-name of Peter Churchill, a former free-lance writer who had won fame by his exploits in the south of France during the previous months when he had established firm contacts with Carte.

In keeping with the cloak-and-dagger image our meeting was suitably dramatic. After dinner that night I repaired to the garden via the back steps on instructions from Bartoli. For some ten minutes or so I hung about in the shadow of a hedge while Bartoli watched from the unlit back door some twenty yards away. Then, at the bottom of the path which led from the sea, a hatless figure appeared, paused and moved rapidly towards me, carrying an umbrella and stooping forward for all the world like Groucho Marx. Raoul had arrived.

Our conversation in the darkness was brief. We discussed sabotage schools and exchanged one or two pleasantries. A few more words of encouragement and then Raoul announced: 'I'll see you later.'

Turning on his heel he disappeared Groucho-like down the path by which he had arrived and in a moment I found myself alone again.

I do not think I saw Peter Churchill more than a couple of times after this meeting, but the walk and the unfurled umbrella remain engraved on my memory. At least no one could say there was anything stereotyped about the appearance of British agents. My own dress most of the time was a sweater and trousers rolled up as I have described, all in keeping with my aluminium bicycle. My fondness for two-wheeled transport was not shared by Sidney Jones, who was still in the area. He became disenchanted after an unfortunate experience one afternoon when he and I took the Bartoli family out for lunch. It was possibly a rash thing to do, for Sidney and I made it a point to avoid being seen together. But we were both bored with inactivity and fed up with living on skimpy rations. The Bartolis, we knew, could have afforded to eat black market style every day if they wished, but André thought that to do so would be unpatriotic. So his family lived on what their humbler countrymen did. It was difficult for him to refuse an invitation to eat with his allies, however, and the Bartolis, children and all, cycled over to join Sidney and I at a restaurant some miles from Cannes.

The meal was excellent. The wine was vintage. The occasion was memorable. Especially for Sidney. For on the road back he braked too quickly as he cycled round a bend. Both his wheels seized. I watched open-mouthed as he soared skywards like an Olympic ski champion, his arms flailing. Then he plummeted head-first to the hard road.

Immediately the Bartolis rushed to his aid, but the sight had been too much for me. I collapsed helpless with laughter while

Sidney, bleeding from a cut on the head, was helped glassy-eyed on to his feet. Tears streamed down my face and my laughter redoubled as he was helped aboard his machine and, with an indignant but dazed look in my direction, wobbled away. Sidney came off best in the end. Madame Bartoli would not speak to me for days afterwards and Sidney was treated like a wounded hero.

The Bartolis had become an important part of our lives. Madame Bartoli we called Madame Magpie, for if I managed to get hold of a bar of chocolate or a tin of milk she would confiscate it and put it away, as she said, 'for a rainy day'. 'You will be glad of this when we fall on hard times.' It never occurred to her that hard times had already arrived.

Her 12-year-old son was a high-spirited boy but it was her youngest daughter who became my favourite. A brown-skinned 14-year-old, when she was not at school Line Bartoli followed me everywhere on her cycle. Sometimes I towed her on her roller skates. On Sunday she bossed me unmercifully, insisting that I should change into my decent suit, shave and tidy myself up and attend Mass with the rest of the family. In return for her companionship, which provided me with a wonderful cover, for no one would suspect a man with a child of being involved in activities against the state, I helped Line with her English studies. Result: her standard of school work plummeted and she was ticked off for slacking. I felt most indignant but I was in no position to complain. Fortunately I was able to fulfil a more useful function when the Italians moved into the area. Their troops, whom the French called Les Pis-Pis, were incorrigible where women were concerned and even a youngster like Line was not safe. The enemy were not the only people Line and I fooled. After lunching with the Bartolis one day I offered to wash up and was standing at the kitchen sink with an apron on when Line arrived and started to tease me. After making one or two blood-curdling threats I seized a broom and, placing it firmly against her wooden sandals propelled her like an ice-skater over the tiled floor while she screamed in mock terror. At that moment the door opened and a strange face peered at us inquisitively. 'I'm sorry,' he said, in an embarrassed and apologetic fashion, 'I was told someone else was in here.'

He turned out to be a distinguished member of S.O.E. who had been asked to contact me on his way inland. What sort of a report he made out when he returned to Orchard Court I never knew. Perhaps he said nothing, on the grounds that no one would ever believe that an intrepid saboteur was larking about with an apron round his middle.

The truth of the matter was that I was under-occupied now that I was acclimatized and too inexperienced to contact the people who were in the best position to advise me. As I had no radio operator of my own, my dealings with London had to be through third parties. And in any case I thought I had nothing of importance to report. Bartoli had told me that André Girard wanted me to go to Corsica to set up a circuit there. Arrangements were being made. I had understood on leaving London that either Girard or Peter Churchill would give me a safe address to go to in Abbeville after I had acclimatized myself in the south, but this was never forthcoming. Not that this upset me, for the idea of actually running my own circuit in Corsica appealed to me, and struck me as being much more exciting than my order to set up in the humble role of sabotage instructor, teaching boring lessons about Stens and time fuses. I wanted to get on with the war and all this hanging around didn't appeal to me.

The idea of going to Corsica was not as wild as it might sound. Corsica was one of the places which had not been directly touched by the battles of 1940. When France surrendered it was still garrisoned by undefeated troops. The Italians who were subsequently sent to occupy it numbered about the same as the Vichy regulars at the end of 1942. And the French still had all their arms.

I waited anxiously for word from London directing me to Corsica and consulted Leonetti, in a cautious manner, on what sort of a place it was. Not unnaturally I assumed that if instructions were forthcoming they would be sent from London to Carte for passing on. When nothing arrived my opinion of undercover work on the Côte d'Azur dropped lower and lower. This was not altogether fair. As the months passed I became very much aware of the complex nature of subversive warfare. There were two schools of thought. One favoured the constant erosion of German morale and the infliction of material damage on the war machine. The other, a more sophisticated approach, aimed at training, equipping and organizing forces which could be called on when the invasion was launched and work with the Allied troops on specific objectives.

The snag with the activist policy was that it was likely to do more harm than good in the long run. Blowing up bridges and murdering German troops was all very well but there were unpleasant side-effects.

Innocent civilians were shot in reprisal. Guards were placed on bridges which had been neglected until then and which would now be harder to tackle when the invasion came. The Germans were also able to assess the strength of Resistance forces in turbulent areas and act accordingly. Instead of being lulled into complacency they were placed on the alert.

Although I was unaware of it, the circuit was already doomed. André Marsac, one of the men who met me when I landed on the beach at Cannes, had been robbed while travelling by train from Marseilles to Paris. His briefcase had fallen into the hands of a German Abwehr* agent. In it was a list of some 200 names of members of the Carte circuit, and included Bartoli. Cleverly the Gestapo bided their time and confined their activities to watching the men named and allowing them to lead them to the members of the organization who had not been listed. Girard's secret army was about to answer its first roll call . . .

These ugly forebodings were happily concealed from me at the time. My mind was taken up with a completely new venture. According to *S.O.E. in France* I was sent to the Riviera with instructions to deliver a message bearing on the proposed escape attempt of General Giraud, at that time a more powerful name in France than that of General de Gaulle. In April 1942 he endeared himself to the French by escaping from his German captors, a feat that was all the more appealing because he had done the same in the First World War. Giraud had a particular advantage over De Gaulle. The Allies believed that he was a genuine counter-attraction to Marshal Pétain as far as the Vichy army was concerned and that his supporters among the regular officers would bring the French forces in the colonies over to our side. His extradition was regarded in 1942 as a vital factor in the battle against the Nazis and had I been entrusted with a message concerning his escape, I

* Security service of the German armed forces, under the command of Admiral Canaris.

would have considered myself honoured indeed. I must confess that this was not the case. My task was a humble one, as I have already described, and I might have continued to cycle round the Riviera to the end of the war, lecturing on Stens and demolition charges, had it not been for a fortuitous meeting with a character known simply as *Le Commandant*.

Le Commandant had been a regular major in the French Army and as far as he was concerned there had been no surrender. About six feet four inches tall and weighing a good fifteen stone, he had gathered about him a band of Resistance fighters who were the terror of the Riviera no matter which side one happened to be on. His *réseau*, or circuit, was known as 'Alliance'. *Le Commandant* was a tough and intelligent man and handled his men well enough although they were a young and impetuous band of desperadoes. He now asked me if I would help him in the execution of a special operation he was planning. I replied that I was very willing to help but that I would have to know a little more about its nature. *Le Commandant* was evasive. The most I could get out of him was that it involved the extrication from France of a *personnage important*. No more would he say at this stage. If I would report to a certain villa near Cannes I could be of the greatest assistance to him.

Two nights later, armed only with a password, I sneaked down the road to the villa and as I drew closer was petrified by the activity going on in the fields and ditches and behind the walls near it. There were little men with long rifles, big men with small pistols, nondescript men with daggers and at least two groups with machine guns. Each of them felt it necessary to prod me with his particular weapon before I was allowed to continue my journey and, as I was only wearing a sweater, my ribs took a considerable pounding. Finally an oily-looking individual with one pistol in his hand and another stuck in his belt grudgingly admitted me to the house. There *Le Commandant*, surrounded by men armed to the teeth, was busy testing a signalling lamp.

I looked round for the *personnage important*, but *Le Commandant* explained that he had not arrived. In any case, I was not there to meet him. I was required to accompany *Le Commandant* to the beach. Why?

'Because we are expecting an English submarine and I will need you to talk to it,' he replied. 'It is to take our important person away with it.'

Clearly he didn't want to tell me more so I didn't press him, but it struck me that there was not much point in the submarine coming if the *personnage* who was so *important* was not already in the house waiting to jump aboard. Often in the war it was better not to know things.

About midnight, after sitting for some time in a darkened room staring out to sea, we tramped out on to the sandy beach, *Le Commandant* clutching his signalling light. His roughnecks remained at their posts, hidden from sight. If we had been better equipped we would have had night glasses – special binoculars for use after dark. As we hadn't we strained our eyes into the blackness. Although it was not cold, condensation formed on my sweater and from time to time I shivered and shrugged my shoulders. *Le Commandant* stamped up and down and beat the palm of his hand with the signal light. Just before dawn we gave up and trailed back to the villa. New guards had taken up positions and the earlier watch littered the living-room of the house, sitting in chairs around the table their heads slumped on their shoulders. Two teenagers in oily dungarees had spread a newspaper over the chintzy fabric of an elegant settee to protect it and were leaning against each other sound asleep. As I opened the door to leave, stale cigarette smoke swirled out after me.

'Tomorrow, then,' said the big man who had kept the vain vigil with me.

'Tomorrow, *mon commandant*.'

He yawned and went back inside. I made my way back to the Bartolis, tired but exhilarated. At last, I thought, things are beginning to shape up. As far as I knew the security of the operation was completely intact. No one in Carte knew anything about it with the possible exception of Bartoli. It was just a matter of time.

The following night was a repeat performance. We saw nothing but the heaving of the calm, unbroken sea and heard only the swish of ripples at the water's edge. I was glad we were waiting on the smooth sands of Cannes and not the cobble-sized pebbles of Nice.

Le Commandant did, however, confide to me the name of the

personnage important for whom the British government was willing to risk yet another submarine. 'We are hiding General Giraud,' he announced with pride. 'It is essential that he joins the Allies now and we will see to it that he does.'

The urgency of the situation, although unknown to ourselves was heightened by the fact that the Allies were on the eve of the invasion of North Africa and Eisenhower considered Giraud vital to his plans. Giraud also had views on who was vital to *his* plans and requested the services of General Chambe, a distinguished French Air Force officer, then reduced to living on half-pay in Lyons. This turned out to be easier said than done, for General Chambe refused to move unless he could take two huge travelling trunks with him. They were for General Giraud, he explained, and vital to the success of the mission. The poor Carte agents, who had strict instructions regarding the amount of baggage a person could take with him, did not know what to do. Finally it turned out that one suitcase contained Giraud's family silver and the other his parade uniforms. There ensued a flaming row and General Chambe departed the way he had come, as indeed did the escape committee.

At this juncture, I came into the picture. As Giraud still insisted on having Chambe as his deputy, I was asked by *Le Commandant* if I would be good enough to go to Lyons and see if the old gentleman would agree to accompany me over the Pyrenees and make his way to Gibraltar via Spain. My acceptance was conditional upon my not having to carry his own suitcases over the mountains!

On 7 November, 1942, the day before the Allied invasion of North Africa, I dressed in my smart Orchard Court clothes and caught the train for Lyons. My forged papers were tucked neatly into my breast pocket and the address of Général de l'Armèe de l'Air Chambe was committed safely to memory. The papers satisfied the routine checks carried out by some bored Vichy officials on the train, I didn't forget the address, and I arrived at Lyons feeling very pleased with myself and delighted to have got away from the slightly unreal atmosphere of the Riviera. Lyons, I had been warned, was a tougher place. It was to get even tougher as the war went on.

Finding General Chambe's flat presented no difficulty. He was not wanted by the authorities and when I rang the bell the door opened almost immediately and I found myself faced with a grey-haired man of medium height, with a beaky, aristocratic nose. He gazed at me with unwavering blue eyes.

'General Chambe?'

'Yes.'

'I have a message for you. May I come in, sir?'

A pause. And then he opened the door and I went in.

'Well?'

'My message is from General Giraud.'

Up to that time his attitude had been cautious and cool. Now he allowed himself to raise his aristocratic eyebrows. By the time I had finished speaking I had been accepted to the point where I was allowed a seat and received the final accolade of being introduced to Madame Chambe, his aged mother, with whom he lived.

She showed absolutely no surprise or emotion whatever when her sixty-year-old son informed her that he was required to join General Giraud in North Africa at once.

'Then you had better go,' she said.

We talked long into the night. He told me that my arrival was a complete surprise; he had made no preparations and would be unable to travel until he had found at least two good staff officers to accompany him. He asked me to return the following day There was no mention of the suitcases!

Obviously he was satisfied with my credentials for when I next saw him he gave me the address of an old friend of his in Toulouse whom I was to contact forthwith and ask for advice on the best way to cross the Pyrenees. If all went well I was to return to Lyons and report. Four days later I was back. His friend, Maître Chesnelong, a distinguished French lawyer, had been unable to get in touch with any escape organization but he did think he could put us in contact with a Spanish guide who would take us across the mountains for a substantial fee. While we were waiting to make our attempt he would be happy to offer his hospitality. Chambe pondered on the problem and then told me to go away and come back in a fortnight.

Dutifully I caught the train south again and resumed my sabotage classes. These had now taken on considerably more significance since the Germans had moved into the so-called Un-occupied Zone at the end of November, as a counter-measure against the Allied invasion of North Africa. Every town on the Riviera swarmed with troops, mostly the despised Italians. The presence of the enemy in such large numbers created an unexpected situation for me as a black marketeer. I found myself beset with demands for dress lengths, soap, cigarette lighters and other things which were scarce in Germany. In fact, had I so wished, I could have retired from my clandestine activities and devoted my time exclusively to this profitable side-line! As it was, I had to work overtime to maintain my reputation as a wide-boy capable of fixing anything for any one. Fortunately I had as an ally the genuine article in the shape of Toto Otoviani, a happy-go-lucky Corsican who provided me with all I needed. On two occasions we even supplied German officers with a few yards of silk and received their grateful thanks as well as their cash. Toto thought it a great joke that a British agent should be supplying his enemies with the luxuries of life.

My black market activities finally extended to a deal on the train to Lyons when I returned to see General Chambe. A keen young Wehrmacht lieutenant had been eyeing me with considerable suspicion and after a while started asking me questions. Where I was going? What was my job? In the end I told him frankly that I was on the black market. Immediately his manner changed. Now there was only one thing on his mind. Could I possibly get him some silk stockings? I said that I would see what I could arrange and at once became his friend for life. He insisted on walking with me from the station and I accompanied him as far as his hotel. A few days later Toto, who was never a man to turn away good money, delivered three pairs of silk stockings.

My visit turned out to be rather disappointing. Chambe was prepared to travel but not his staff officers. They had not completed their arrangements and I was required to postpone the trip until after Christmas. I returned to the Riviera somewhat irritated and arrived just in time to witness a remarkable feat by my old comrade *Le Commandant*. I had gone to Nice in the hope of contacting him and was standing by the window in a flat on the Avenue des Anglais when *Le Commandant* himself shot past on the pillion of a tiny motorcycle. Looking like an angry bear, and absolutely dwarfing the machine and the driver, he disappeared in a cloud of dust and petrol fumes. Minutes later a crowd of excited gendarmes roared up the road in pursuit in a lorry.

I learned that *Le Commandant* had been captured and taken under escort to the *gendarmerie*. At the entrance he noticed one of his faithful followers waiting nearby with a motorcycle. *Le Commandant* didn't need telling twice and was gone before the gendarmes knew what had happened.

6

Le Commandant's escape was a piece of good news I was able to take with me when I made another visit to Lyons just before the New Year. Chambe also had good news for me – he and his staff officers were ready to move in a day or two. The arrangements were simple. We bought our tickets at intervals so that they could not of themselves prove any connection between us. The officers said goodbye to their families, the general to his mother and I sent a message to the Bartolis to say that I would not be seeing them for some time. They knew that I was due to return to England but by what means they had no idea. Madame Bartoli made me a present of a beautiful little smock dress for my baby daughter. The dress travelled with me stuffed into my jacket pocket.

The journey to Toulouse was uneventful. Our party split up so that each one travelled in a different coach, and there was no trouble with our papers. Since the war I have read many accounts of the tense moment when a Gestapo or a police official carefully studies the documents of a secret agent. All I can say is that someone must have found some very strange trains. Most of those I travelled in were packed to the roof and the opportunity for any official to study papers properly simply didn't exist. Usually some harrassed bespectacled individual squinted myopically at one's papers, grunted and handed them back. My papers must have been asked for thirty or forty times – yet never once was I challenged. Forgeries were one thing that Orchard Court did to perfection. Only prison camp escapers who had manufactured their passes on home-made presses, or had faked stolen ones, were likely to be picked up. The real time to worry was when the Gestapo had been tipped off that there was an agent on a train. Then they would meet it in force at a station and passengers would have to pass through special barriers. On such occasions it was quite normal for some poor fellow who could not satisfy the questioners as to his identity to be taken away for 'further examination'. Generally this meant that his description had been given to the police beforehand.

At Toulouse we left the train separately. The staff officers went to stay with friends. Chambe and I met at the home of Maître Chesnelong.

The lawyer was delighted to see his old friend. I was equally pleased to learn that he had found a guide or *passeur* for us. When I saw this individual next day at a town about twelve miles from Toulouse I was not so pleased. He was quite prepared to take us to the border, he said, but once we were there we would be on our own. He did not wish to end up in Miranda, the notorious Spanish concentration camp where Franco kept captured escapers. Although his pessimism cast a slight doubt on the adventure I agreed to meet him at a farm about fifteen miles from the foot of the Pyrenees the following afternoon, and Chambe approved these arrangements when I reported back.

Dinner that evening was a bit of a strain, not because of what lay ahead of us as much as what Madame Chesnelong put in front of us. She had done her best, but feeding two extra mouths as well as her husband, two sons and a daughter, meant the provision of a very frugal meal indeed. Maître Chesnelong, anxious to make some gesture for his old friend's sake, eventually produced a precious cigar for the general after we had been served our ersatz coffee. Gallantly the general, who recognized the sacrifice being made, excused himself with the remark:

'Never a good cigar unless one has had a good dinner first.'

There was a moment's awkward silence and then the assembled company burst out laughing. Maître Chesnelong insisted and the general had his cigar after all. It was just as well, for there was precious little in the way of comfort in the days immediately ahead.

We set out by train early next morning, still travelling in different compartments. Near Bayonne we got out at separate stations so as not to attract attention and made our way to a large hut where we were to assemble. Everything went according to plan and I handed over part of the money to our guide. He was to receive the balance when we reached the border.

'We move at 10 p.m.,' was all he said.

As we sat about on piles of fodder I was able to take stock of my companions. The two staff officers could have been twins. They were young, dark, about medium height and sported clipped moustaches. Both wore thick belted overcoats. Our guide, a swarthy, chunky little man was also well wrapped up and had a knapsack on his back. *Mon Général* looked absolutely dashing in what was called a *canadienne*, a fur-lined olive-green jacket with a fur collar. Breeches, knee boots and a stout cap completed his dress and he looked like a *Boy's Own Paper* drawing of a lumber-jack. When I asked him if he felt he would be all right he replied:

'Don't worry about me, my boy. In the mountains I am like a *coq de bruyère* (a grouse). You ought to look to yourself. You are not exactly dressed for the crossing, are you?'

He was right. I was still wearing my best black market suit and highly polished low shoes. The weather had been quite pleasant when I left the Riviera. Here, in the foothills, there was a distinct nip in the air. I hoped it wouldn't snow.

The minutes ticked away and as night closed in the gloom of the hut deepened, obscuring our faces in shadow. Outside we could hear the occasional barking of farm dogs, otherwise all was silent. From time to time the flaring of a match threw a ruddy glow on the face of the smoker.

'It's time to go, messieurs,' said our guide at last, heaving himself to his feet, and we shook ourselves from our torpor.

The air was cold and the sky clear as we tramped in single file by the side of the road, like an infantry section on the march. The general strode behind the guide and I brought up the rear. Here and there patches of frost gleamed in the moonlight. Only the guide spoke and then just to warn us of any change of direction. Every hour or so we halted for five minutes. At one of these stops our guide informed us that we had crossed into the *Zone Interdite* – the Forbidden Zone which ran some 25 kilometres deep along the coast line. If we were caught now our papers would be useless as one had to have special passes and there were strict regulations about movements in the area. Anyone suspected of improperly penetrating the Zone could expect real trouble. I derived some comfort from the fact that our guide had taken us past the guard posts without us even seeing them.

Gradually the sky lightened and the black mass of the hills ahead took on various shades of grey. On the crests of the ridges and the lower slopes ominous white patches warned of snow ahead. Towards dawn I found myself searching my pockets for surviving fragments of the bread I had brought with me but discovered that I had eaten the lot. I cheered myself up by making sure that the baby's dress was still there. The material felt warm and soft. Suddenly four gendarmes on bicycles appeared just where the road swept over the brow of a hill and pedalled purposefully towards us. I looked round but the countryside was uncharitably bare of cover. There was only one thing we could do.

'Keep going,' I called. 'They may not bother about us.'

I turned out to be optimistic. The gendarmes rode to within ten yards and then dismounted. A burly sergeant and one of the men propped up their bicycles and came towards us. The other two watched from a distance.

'Papiers,' demanded the sergeant of General Chambe.

He received a cool stare in reply. No one spoke.

'Very well, messieurs, I am afraid we will have to ask you to accompany us to the *gendarmerie*,' said the sergeant. 'Perhaps you will give us your explanation there.'

There was nothing to do but obey. The gendarmes were armed and we did not have a peashooter between us. With the sergeant leading the way we trudged two or three miles up a side road to a village and were led into the office of the *gendarmerie*.

There, having removed his coat and his kepi, the sergeant donned a solemn expression, settled himself behind a table and tapped purposefully with a pencil on a report form. His minions, still fully dressed with their hats on, looked on admiringly, blocking the door behind us.

'Now,' said the sergeant gravely, 'you must explain just what you are doing here.'

Once more a stony silence greeted his question.

'I warn you, you are in a very serious situation. This is the *Zone*

Interdite. If you have not got a good reason for being here ...'

One of the young staff officers shifted his feet uncomfortably and the sergeant stabbed in his direction with the pencil.

'You were going to say something, monsieur?'

The officer was about to reply when he saw Chambe's cold blue eyes on him. He choked back whatever he had been going to say.

'Very well,' said the sergeant, 'we will have to lock you up and send for the captain.'

The watching gendarmes shook their heads pityingly, as if the Devil himself were about to descend on us.

I decided that the situation was getting out of hand.

'*Mon sergent*,' I said threateningly, 'I should think very carefully before doing anything which you may regret in the future. Your career depends on your actions today.'

He stopped tapping his pencil. Steal a gendarme's wife but do not threaten his promotion.

'What do you mean? Explain yourself.'

'Well, naturally sergeant,' I said, 'it is up to you,' (at this recognition of his authority he nodded condescendingly), 'but you must realize that there are cases which can be dealt with only by the highest officials. And this is one.'

His eyes narrowed and the audience drew in their breath sharply.

'I must speak to someone in the highest authority as soon as possible,' I repeated firmly. Then, allowing anger to creep into my voice, continued:

'If you do not carry out my request as soon as possible I will be unable to avoid making an official complaint of your treatment in detaining these important gentlemen in a manner which I can only say is highly irregular.'

I sensed the sergeant's feeling that perhaps there was something unpleasant hanging over him. My Paris accent, the haughty attitude of Chambe and the military bearing of the staff officers puzzled and impressed him. His confederates looked on, fascinated to see what their leader would do. The sergeant realized it was his great chance and he took it. The French love a dramatic situation and who was he to spoil the atmosphere? Rising to his feet he struck a deliberate pose, arms on his hips.

'Very well, monsieur,' he replied. 'I will take you to the mayor of Licq. Jean-Claude, prepare the car.'

If the other gendarmes could have applauded I am sure they would have done so. The ultimate deterrent had been produced. My bluff had been called.

Only when I replied, 'Excellent, just the man I want to see,' did they realize that the situation was now entirely out of their control. The sergeant made a lame effort to regain the initiative by saying he could take only one of us to see the mayor.

I hit back by saying that on no account would I leave my friends at the *gendarmerie* and that if they were not taken immediately to the local inn there would be more trouble.

After a moment or two's hesitation he agreed and, slightly bewildered, Chambe, his staff and the *passeur* were ushered respectfully out. The sergeant, one of the gendarmes and I climbed into an ancient Citroën and drove off.

On the journey the sergeant became much more relaxed and persuasive. 'You can tell me, surely, monsieur,' was his approach. But I would say nothing. He knew no more about us when we arrived at Licq in the middle of the afternoon, some forty miles from where we were picked up, than when we set out.

At the *mairie* we waited outside the office of the mayor in a corridor full of brown-varnished doors and a peculiar smell of mothballs. A clerk told us that we would not be kept long. After ten minutes a tall, pleasant-looking man in his late thirties put his head out of the door and said 'Come in.' The sergeant made as if to accept the invitation then caught my eye and took up a position on guard outside.

I decided not to beat about the bush. The mayor looked a decent type and struck me as probably being a rugby player – the game is very popular in that part of France and some of the best players come from there.

'*Monsieur le maire*,' I said, 'I am a British officer. The old gentleman is General Chambe and the two men with him are his staff officers. It is imperative that we should cross the mountains to join General Giraud in North Africa. Can you help us?'

You would have thought he dealt with such requests every day of his life. After I had outlined our intentions he replied:

61

'But, of course, just tell me what I can do.'

'Simply let us go on our way,' I said. 'That way will be best for everyone.'

Actually there was no other way of crossing except by *passeur* as all other traffic through the *Zone Interdite* was screened with a fine tooth comb.

'Very well. Sergeant!'

An expectant face shot round the door.

'Sir?'

'Take monsieur back to his friends.'

And as the eyebrows of the gendarme shot up he added: *'Donnez leurs carte blanche.'* The way was clear.

On the way back in the car I tried to sleep and so did the baffled sergeant. His last words before he dozed off were: *'Vous êtes vernis.'* Literally translated that meant I had been varnished (with luck). A more colloquial English translation would be 'Jammy bastard . . .'

We arrived back at the *gendarmerie* at 4 a.m. and roused the slumbering duty officer. He was immediately sent to fetch Chambe and his aides, who appeared blinking the sleep from their eyes ten minutes later.

'It's all right, *mon général,*' I said cheerfully, 'we're on our way.'

He beamed, his two staff officers looked distinctly depressed and the sergeant smirked as if it had been all his own doing.

As we set off in the half-light he shook his head and whispered again: *'Vous êtes vernis.'*

The sergeant was right. We were 'jammy bastards' to get out of such a mess. What would have happened had we been held in the cells was indisputable. The Gestapo did not have enough men to call at remote villages every day, so they instituted calls, say, twice a week when any strangers in the cells were taken off for 'questioning'. The Gestapo were due on their rounds the next day – which would have meant a concentration camp for the Frenchmen and probably curtains for me.

With this in mind we took much greater care during the rest of our approach march to the mountains, continually stopping and sending one of our number on if we were not sure of what lay ahead. Fortunately thick woods on the lower French slopes enabled us to leave the road and travel by daylight. By the time we left this cover it was dark. Stumbling over rocks, slipping on the steep hillside we clambered upwards, the snow getting deeper all the time. My clothes became saturated and my shoes torn. From time to time one of us would plunge into a hollow filled with fine snow and almost disappear. It reached ankle height, knee height and at one point I was wading through it up to my waist. Despite everything I felt more hungry than tired. As for Chambe, true to his word and unlike his officers he went up that mountain like a *coq de bruyère*. The officers complained bitterly of exhaustion; they wanted to know what was going to happen when we reached the border and the *passeur* left us. Frequently they stopped to rest.

The *passeur* remained stolidly indifferent and maintained a good pace so that we should reach the border before dawn.

On we went, scrambling on hands and knees over gullies and crevices, splashing through icy streams, clinging and tugging at stunted undergrowth to pull ourselves up steep ridges. It was well after sun-up that the guide stopped and announced we had crossed the border. From now on we were on our own.

What he really meant was that Chambe and I were on our own. The two young officers had had enough. They had discussed things at one of the halts on the way and decided there was no chance of getting past the Spanish frontier patrols in daylight and they were too worn out to wait until the following night. They would go back with the guide, they said, and try to join the general later. I handed over what we owed to the *passeur* in silence and shame-facedly the two officers turned away. Chambe said nothing but looked hurt and angry. The guide, imperturbable as ever, merely pointed and said that if we carried on for a few miles we would hit a road. As an afterthought he advised us to keep off the sky-line and not to descend in a direct line but to cut across the face of the mountain at a tangent to avoid being seen. We thanked him and set off towards a stretch of thinly-spaced trees where at least we would have some cover.

Compared with the French side of the mountain the Spanish slopes were warm and pleasant. There was no sign of snow; there was no sign of anything or anyone. In the woods General Chambe halted and held what he called a *conseil de guerre*. He was a resilient old man and refused to be put out by any snags. I honestly believe he was enjoying himself.

'It's no good heading for that road, my friend,' he said. 'That leads only to one place . . . Miranda. And I have no wish to spend the war there.'

I agreed wholeheartedly. 'Let's take a chance,' I suggested, 'and try to get someone to take a message to the nearest British consul, wherever he may be?' The general saw no objection, and an hour and a half later we found our man. He was carrying a rifle slung across one shoulder and had a large bag across the other. Bits and pieces of equipment, including a large knife, festooned a grubby green uniform. He was bending earnestly over something on the ground with his back towards us when we spotted him, but when we were some twenty-five yards away he swung round with a start. I don't know what he was expecting but when he saw us he stood up and scratched his head.

Our new acquaintance turned out to be the Spanish equivalent of the French *garde forestier*, a game warden, out hunting. A jolly, fat little man with a weatherbeaten countenance, he accepted us at once as friends in need. We wanted shelter? He would find it. We wanted food? He would provide it. We wanted the British consul? That was a little more difficult . . . but not to worry. He would do his best.

Manuel, for that was his name, was as good as his word. By mid-afternoon Chambe and I were ensconced in a roomy cave in the middle of the woods dining on cold venison. This washed down with a bottle of rough red wine made us feel new men. Only our filthy condition bothered us, as we had not shaved since we left Toulouse nor had we washed. We attempted a toilette in a freezing stream which ran through a clearing in front of the cave but with little effect.

The following day Manuel visited us twice with venison but without news of any contact. On the third day after our arrival he appeared early in the morning with a large supply of meat and bread and told us that he would be gone for some time. We were not to light any fires in his absence and we were to expect him back some time the following evening. Sure enough at the appointed time he returned with another man, who introduced himself as a doctor and an Anglophile. He was at our service. As soon as he had heard what we wanted he was off again, promising to be back as quickly as he could. About thirty-six hours later he returned, bringing with him a section of a map and a map reference. Then, without ceremony, he was gone and with him our deer-hunting benefactor.

The general and I set out in pursuit of the map-reference and after four hours of trekking through the woods, emerged from the undergrowth at the side of a road. Two men were sitting in a parked car which bore a C.D. plate. They were unmistakably English. Getting up from the thicket I walked towards them followed by my companion, now a white-bearded scarecrow in tattered knee boots.

'Glad to see you,' said a cheerful voice as I introduced myself. 'Who's your friend?'

'This is General Chambe,' I replied. 'It is important that he should rejoin General Giraud as quickly as possible.'

By evening we were in the British Embassy in Barcelona where I wasted no time in getting into a hot bath. The water was the blackest I have ever seen, before or since, but as the dirt of the Pyrenees disappeared down the plughole I felt as fit as . . . a *coq de bruyère*. The journey from Toulouse to Barcelona in nine days was, I understood, a record!

After my bath I sat once more in a borrowed dressing-gown while my indestructible spiv's suit was cleaned and pressed.

The baby's dress, which had been found crumpled and filthy in my pocket, was returned, spotless, by an inscrutable valet.

Two days later I was flown to Algiers and taken to the palace where General Giraud had set up his headquarters. Still in my black marketeer's suit I was led in past French colonial troops in turbans, splendid officers with white kepis and elegant staff captains bustling about the palm-dotted courtyards. For an hour I hung about waiting for the summons, and growing steadily more annoyed. Finally, just as I was thinking of sending in my apologies and leaving, an emissary arrived and led me to the General's office. A tall, fine-looking man, he shook my hand so warmly that any irritation melted away. He congratulated me on my service to his comrade, General Chambe, and paid tribute to my '*perspicasité*'. Finally he produced, seemingly from up his sleeve, a medal with a green and red ribbon which he said was the Croix de Guerre awarded to him in the 1914–18 War and pinned it on my suit, following it up by embracing me. Not having a clue what to do, I stood stiffly to attention and, after a further handshake, left with the medal still pinned to my manly chest. Once outside the room I hastily unfastened it and thrust it into my pocket before fleeing through the general's curious entourage.

From Algiers I was flown to Lisbon – the direct flight to England being too dangerous non-stop – where I won £40 in the casino at Estoril before catching the plane home. A kindly steward changed the escudos into sterling which he handed me when I went aboard. I felt that I was indeed a jammy bastard.

7

O F all the troublesome pieces of advice I received from
S.O.E. the worst was to have nothing to do with women.
Women, I was told, were dangerous. Women spelled ruin. What
was not revealed to me was the fact that if a man conditions himself to ignore them completely and doesn't even think of sex, it
will adversely affect his legitimate love life in the end. During my
whole sojourn in France I had taken the warnings of my master
literally and apart from matrons of mature years and girls young
enough to be my daughters, I had no conversation with females.
The result: I was completely impotent.

Not unnaturally this caused some consternation when Tiny arrived in answer to my message asking her to join me at the S.O.E.
hotel in Kensington. Searching questions were asked, and it was
only with the greatest difficulty that I managed to convince her
that it was indeed a shortage, and not a surfeit, of feminine
company from which I was suffering!

I had so completely soaked myself in the character of Jean Delannoy, whom I had made into a celibate bachelor that it took
some time for me to resume my real identity. The proof that I was
two people is illustrated by the difference between the passport
photograph taken before I set off for Gibraltar and the one taken
when I flew back. The face may be the same but the personality is
completely different. Fortunately the threat to my married life was
only temporary and harmony was restored along with my true
identity.

I was dreading the task of explaining to Tiny that my stay was
only a short one, for I felt that in some way I was letting her down.
But it had to be done. In the end, after I'd had a bath and was

washing my hair I felt suitably protected by a lather of suds to say, 'I'm awfully sorry darling, but I've got to go back on the next moon.' There was an ominous silence, then a sigh. But when I wiped the soap from my eyes Tiny just gave a forced grin and said: 'If that's the case we had better celebrate while we can. Where are you taking me to dinner tonight?' I have seldom felt more relieved.

Why the hurry? It was simply that Orchard Court were a little too pleased with my report. A car had taken me there immediately I landed and I had been ushered straight into a room where Buckmaster and Jepson were waiting. Both were delighted and Buckmaster, whom I would hardly describe as demonstrative, actually shook me by the hand. Then I was taken to meet Major-General Colin Gubbins, regarded by most informed people as the mainspring of S.O.E. I found myself in the presence of a cocky, sturdy little man with a mass of medal ribbons, who expressed his pleasure with my work and told me that he expected great things of me. He gave the impression of having boundless energy and later in the war he proved it to me. Having seen him enter a F.A.N.Y. (First Aid Nursing Yeomanry) Mess for a ten-minute chat about eleven o'clock in the evening I discovered him doing hand stands in the same place at five o'clock the following morning.

After receiving Gubbins's benediction I reported back to be briefed for my forthcoming tasks and it was then I learned that I was to go back to France in about a week, as soon as the moon was suitable for a Lysander operation.

What London wanted to know was just how strong were the claims put forward by Giraud and Chambe about the strength of the support promised by former French officers. Did the reported groups or the so-called secret army really exist? If so how could they best be helped? If they did exist, I was to make sure that the arms and the money they were to get were not wasted.

My contact in France was to be Commandant Lejeune, code-name Delphin, who would fly out with me and whose wireless operator would send my findings to England. I would not have an operator with me but I would have my own one-time code – a silk pad of figures which corresponds to one held by your base each leaf of which is destroyed after use. This suited me as it meant my messages could not be read by Delphin if they were critical of the Giraudists and the Secret Army. But action through him meant that I would have the added risk of contacting him in Paris, a Gestapo hotbed.

I was given two further tasks. One was to deliver a cheque for, I think, four million francs, to a director of the casino at Monte Carlo, whom I was to meet in Paris. This the British Government guaranteed to cash after the war in return for the credit he would extend. To ensure the validity of the cheque a code message of confirmation was to be broadcast over the B.B.C.'s Radio France Parlent aux Français. Only then would the cheque be valid.

The cheque was concealed between the layers of leather which went to make up the heel of my left shoe, a job the experts at Orchard Court did remarkably well but, as we shall see, without any great forethought. This, however, was not all I was required to deliver. A letter from General Giraud to Madame Giraud was also given to me to hand over to a courier in Paris. The danger of being found with such a letter in my possession was self-evident but it was felt that he was too important a man to say no to, so my handicap went up still further in the Gestapo stakes.

As on my first tour of duty my code-name remained Valentin, and my cover story was unchanged. I was still Jean Delannoy – which, translated, really means 'The Nut'. My suit, I'm glad to say, was changed and I settled for a sports jacket with huge padded shoulders and a narrow waist. In view of the amount of hanging about I'd experienced previously I also selected a very thick roll-neck sweater from S.O.E.'s wardrobe and even obtained one for Lionel Cecil, my wife's brother-in-law, who was reported months later to have become so enamoured of it that he slept in it and took it off only to clean his boots with it.

My parting gifts from S.O.E. were the traditional phial of poison for the lapel of my jacket, a .38 Walther pistol, in case the reception committee turned out to be gentlemen in long coats and felt hats, and a pair of solid gold cuff links. These were a personal good-luck present from Buckmaster and I am told that he gave them to a number of agents. Although they suited my role as a flashy character, I hoped that he did not dole them out to agents acting the parts of men in humbler stations in life. They were probably not a very sensible idea, despite the good intentions of the donor.

Although *I* had been assured of the urgent nature of the 'op', no one had managed to convince the moon and on the night I was supposed to set off a motor-cyclist stopped our car with its drawn blinds half-way to Tangmere where Lejeune and I were to join our plane. We drove back to London where I was reunited with my wife barely six hours after she had kissed me a fond farewell. The following morning I reported to Orchard Court and was told that there would be 'No op tonight'. What better excuse to take my wife, and John Young's, to the Berkeley for lunch. There, just as I was enjoying a glass of brandy, a young lady in F.A.N.Y. uniform appeared to inform me that the operation was on. She had tracked me from my sister-in-law's flat to Fortnum and Mason's where my sister-in-law was shopping, thence to the Berkeley dining-room, where she identified me by my description. I certainly embarked on my mission having eaten and drunk very well.

Lejeune and I left by Lysander on 17 March and landed in a field near Poitiers. The flight took about four hours, and was un-eventful although cramped. The Lysander was on the ground no longer than four minutes during which time Lejeune and I got out with our suitcases and outgoing agents took our places. Another Lysander which landed at the same place did the same thing in the same time. The organizer of this remarkable piece of air traffic control was Henri Déricourt, a former French airline pilot who was later suspected of being a double-agent working for the Germans and sent for trial after the war. Although he was acquitted, mainly on evidence supplied by senior S.O.E. representatives, the stigma remained. I can only say that I regarded him as being outstanding in his field and I did not hesitate to trust him with my own life at any time. As no agents were lost at his receptions his record would seem to speak for itself. As for the argument that the Germans were happy to let agents land as long as Déricourt was trusted by Orchard Court, I note that the Gestapo had no such scruples in Holland where more than forty agents were put straight into the bag after being met by rigged reception committees.

On the night that Lejeune and I arrived my only criticism of the arrangements was that he got to the bicycles first. His was obviously the property of a heavyweight gendarme for he rode off into the night perched on it like a mahout on an elephant. Mine must have been stolen from some undersized child or a circus dwarf. It was ludicrously small and any Gestapo man watching me pedal down the moonlit lanes of Vienne with my knees rising at an obtuse angle in order to avoid the handlebars would have been unable to shout 'Halte' for laughing.

I took the opportunity on this journey of disposing of my Walther .38 in the first suitable ditch as I had no wish to be forced to explain away a gun if I were stopped. Pistols always seemed to me an unecessary part of an ordinary agent's equipment. My poison phial went the same way.

Lejeune and I met as arranged at a safe house about five or six miles from the landing ground and shared a bed there for the rest of the night. In the morning we made our separate ways to Paris by train, having agreed to meet at the Café des Sports at the Porte Maillot the following day.

As usual the train was crowded and the journey most uncomfortable. Giraud's letter bothered me, and soon after the train started I decided to let it travel on its own. Pushing my way to the lavatory I eased it carefully behind the mirror over the washbasin and left it there. As the train approached Paris I returned to the lavatory to retrieve the confounded document. Unfortunately the motion of the train had shaken it down slightly and I was still struggling to extract it with a pin when we drew into the station. Mercifully a final despairing effort harpooned the letter, which I then wrapped round my ankle inside my sock in case I was searched as I left the station. It was a great relief when I finally handed it over for onward transmission to Madame Giraud in Lyons.

However, the problems of being a postman with secret mail were not over yet. There was also the question of the cheque in the heel of my shoe. Orchard Court had done a magnificent job in putting it there but no one had thought about getting it out. I tried with a knife but the leather was too tough. I tried levering off the heel with a screwdriver, but I stopped for fear of damaging the cheque. In the end I had to use a hammer and chisel as best I could before the wretched piece of paper was brought to light. This created another problem – the repair of the shoe. It was impossible to walk into a shop and buy another pair so I had to concoct some yarn about catching my heel in a grid at the base of a tree set in the pavement and wait while the cobbler replaced it on the spot.

Paris was a dangerous place to linger in. There were too many traitors and Gestapo men about, apart from scores of German troops either on leave or serving in the garrison. The latter, from what I saw of them, were no problem and behaved correctly and normally. I got the impression that the ordinary German soldier would behave as he was told by his superiors. If civilized conduct was the order of the day he would act decently. Conversely if he was told to wreck a house or play the brutal conqueror he would obey just as efficiently. Anyway the sight of them on the streets of Paris was offensive to me, however they conducted themselves. I was glad to leave when I had finished my business three days later.

The task of assessing the value of the Giraudist secret army was not an easy one. Most of the ex-regular officers involved seemed to find it very difficult to turn their minds to clandestine and subversive activities. The security of many of them was appalling. It was as if they were trying to play at soldiers in plain clothes. Precautions suggested by trained agents were received sceptically.

People like *Le Commandant*, who had been involved in the operation to rescue Giraud, were the exception. Many officers were arrested because they went about their business too blatantly. Several of them made the mistake of repeatedly holding large meetings at their houses. Others simply faded out of the picture because they were not prepared to put in the tremendous amount of routine work which is needed in the training of men in secret. Some quit because they could not see the day arriving when the lessons taught would be put into practice. To teach a group of fifty men in classes of five at a time for a job which they might not be required to do for eighteen months or two years seemed farcical to the more adventurous. The theory of guerilla warfare was a bore. They demanded action and proof that it worked. One major in Lyons proved to be particularly stubborn. He simply refused to believe that a small amount of plastic explosive could do the destruction I claimed it could. He insisted on a demonstration. His team, two sergeants and two soldiers from the disbanded French army, added their voices to his appeals. In the end I gave in, although I warned them it was the height of stupidity to stick our necks out, particularly mine. To make the operation as safe as I could I selected a stretch of railway line about twelve kilometres from Lyons. For two weeks we went over the plan and practised with our plastic explosive, the major stating his disbelief again and again that what was to him a minute amount of P.E. could do the job. Came the night and we placed three charges at intervals of five yards and retired to a waiting car which I had laid on for a prompt retreat. We sat in silence, the major hanging out of the open window with his ear cocked. At the time the charges should have gone off nothing happened. The darkened countryside stretched peacefully around us, its silence unbroken. A gentle spring wind rustled the poplars lining the road. After five minutes more of tranquillity the major put his head inside the car and stared sulkily ahead. Another five minutes and he turned a face, moonlike in the gloom, and began a reproachful speech. As he did so a brilliant flash lit the car and a noise somewhere between a crack and a clang rippled over the fields. The time pencils had done their job after all and the major became delirious with the joy of actually having achieved something. His hand shot to the door handle.

'Where the hell do you think you are going,' I asked him.

'I must see what we have done, Jean,' he replied. 'I will be gone only a minute.'

'You'll be gone for ever if you don't shut up,' I told him and ordered our driver to get out of it fast.

A report the following day from friendly railway sources revealed that we had blown up ten yards of track. From the point of view of morale this worked wonders for the major and his men; but in the long term such actions were apt to do more harm than good. Isolated incidents of this nature led in many cases to reprisals by the Germans and the deaths of many innocent people. Blown bridges were always repaired, railway lines replaced and roads mended. Worse still, the crack of exploding P.E. served as a warning gong to the Germans to look to their defences and made things harder for everyone when the right time came. The argument that it was better to lull the enemy into a false sense of security and strike only when the secret army was called out *en masse* cut no ice, however, with the great majority of French resisters. As a consequence Gestapo activity intensified, particularly in the Lyons area.

An increasing number of officers were arrested. What happened to at least one of them I saw for myself. Coming out of the station one day I was crossing the road with a crowd when I heard a splintering of glass and looking up saw a body hurtling to the ground from the third floor of a tall building. The crowd surged towards the crumpled figure on the pavement and gasped with horror. The man who lay there in his shirt sleeves had been killed by the fall all right but the injuries which made him such a ghastly sight had been caused by something else. There were burns on his bared chest, slashes on his face and one of his eyes had been almost gouged out.

A door flew open and half a dozen men ran from the doors of the building into the street towards the corpse, shouting and swearing. In a flash the crowd scattered. I had already walked on. It did not take more than a glance to identify the handiwork of the Gestapo from whose headquarters the latest victim of torture had leaped. Later I heard that he was a Giraudist officer who had chosen to commit suicide when he realized he was on the point of giving the Gestapo the information they demanded.

Such incidents should have filled me with hate. But this was something I could not afford to indulge in. Hate is too conspicuous. It was my job to maintain a completely nondescript personality under all circumstances and I worked hard at it for the sake of my neck as much as anything. To have allowed the sight of Germans to evoke any response would have been fatal and so I learned to look at them quite dispassionately.

Although my area of operations included Lyons, Clermont Ferrand, Marseilles and Nice, I made my headquarters with Maître Chesnelong in Toulouse. This meant that I had to do a considerable amount of travelling by train and one of the first moves I made was to apply, in the normal way, for a pass. Toto Otaviani, with whom I had re-established contact, pulled a few strings and in no time at all I had a genuine document authorizing me to travel between various areas without any close questions being asked. As a further precaution I always travelled first class and, whenever it was possible, chose a compartment where there were German officers. As no patriotic Frenchman would have been seen in the company of the Boche, I was immediately regarded by the enemy as at least friendly and when the inspectors and police came round the train they frequently did not trouble me even for my identity papers. Half the time they assumed that I was a member of the Gestapo myself. The more the heat was turned on the nearer the Germans I tried to get. After I saw the officer fall to his death at Lyons for example, I spent the night in a swimming-pool-cum-Turkish-bath, sleeping after my massage. All around me the Wehrmacht snored heartily.

Security had become an obsession and the desire to merge my character entirely with that of Jean Delannoy was almost compulsive. I ignored the instructions about having nothing to do with women and took a girl-friend in Toulouse. After a time it became impossible to conceal from her just what I was and I took her into my confidence, at least to some extent. She was quite aware that I had a wife in England and that when I assumed my real identity I would no longer be hers. But she accepted it.

'To me you are just Jean Delannoy,' she said. 'He is the man I love. If he does not return from his travels some day, I will be suffering no more than thousands of other women in France who wait in hope.'

Women may regard my behaviour as heartless. And, in a purely romantic way, it was. However I was concerned not with love but with survival. And I did not deceive the girl. I did not force her to sleep with me. She came to my bed knowing full well that our affair was an ephemeral thing and that any moment I might be transformed into a stranger. For my part, I was able to remain confident that because I had at least been truthful I would be spared the wrath of a woman scorned if the worst ever happened. As for my wife, the man who returned to her (if he was lucky enough to do so) would be no different from the one who had left her. John Goldsmith and Jean Delannoy were different people. One was a married Englishman with a wife and family in England. The other was a Frenchman, a bachelor with a sweetheart in France.

The only thing I would have regarded as being wrong was the possibility of allowing my French love affair to distract me from my work and I had no intention of letting that happen. Other agents who had allowed love to become entangled in their affairs were now in gaol – or dead.

For weeks I travelled over the area assigned to me, spotting suitable landing grounds and dropping zones and meeting officers who might be prepared to join the secret army. Occasionally I used a car, but never unless the driver had a good reason for being where we were. Apart from being stopped from time to time by patrols of Germans with dogs there was little to worry about. Under the tranquil surface, however, the pot was beginning to boil.

Now the Gestapo, having played a cat and mouse game long enough with the Carte organization, moved in. Arrest after arrest was made. Luckily forty of the men named in the documents found in Marsac's briefcase were warned by a local police chief of the forthcoming swoop and were able to make themselves scarce. Bartoli went into hiding in the house of a friend in Antibes, took the name of Adrien Battesti, and posed as a painter. Being a good amateur in water-colours this was not difficult.

André Girard, the head of Carte, escaped to England and eventually to the U.S.A. His wife was put in a concentration camp, an ordeal which she survived with heroic bravery. Carte's fall brought down other circuits with which it had made contact. Paris in particular became a dangerous place. Henri Frager's organization, Jean-Marie, was penetrated after he associated with Colonel Henri, a notorious Abwehr double-agent, and Frager himself was seized and taken to Germany. This brave but impetuous man paid for his recklessness with his head. He was decapitated.

So many people were cornered in restaurants and cafés that I chose to defy the training instructions I had received and used instead the Bois de Boulogne or the Parc Monceau. As any viewer of television thrillers knows, parks are obvious places for spies to hand over documents. And this is probably quite true. The Gestapo and the Abwehr were constant visitors to the parks of Paris. But they couldn't arrest every stroller and they were quite likely to have become bored with abortive patrols. And so I arranged with Lejeune that when we agreed to meet, say at ten o'clock in the morning this meant that we would be there an hour later. Furthermore we would not meet on the hour but five minutes afterwards.

In this way if anyone did get to know of our meeting they would be there to catch us an hour before we arrived. The idea of the Gestapo hanging about on what appeared to be a false tip for an hour was highly unlikely. What is more, if they got there first their long grey-green coats and gangster hats would be visible for all to see.

Confidently, therefore, I bade my girl-friend goodbye and caught the train for Paris and another meeting with Lejeune to make arrangements for meeting certain army officers. Her last words were:

'Au revoir, mon amour.' She did not realize it but it was also goodbye.

8

As the list of arrests and 'blown' circuits grew, I redoubled my precautions.

Sometimes danger threatened from the quarter where it was least expected. One night in the early summer I was travelling by train near Clermont-Ferrand when an air-raid or some trouble on the line forced it to stop. It halted in open country for more than an hour and, as it had been made quite plain that it would be some time before it got moving again, I got out to stretch my legs. All sorts of people, German and French, were climbing down and doing the same. Unbelievably I bumped into someone in the gloom and recognized Brian Rafferty, a dare-devil young Irishman whom I had met in England. He was working a sabotage group in the area and operated under the code-name Dominique. Without thinking he laughed and said in English, 'Fancy meeting you here . . .', and he continued to talk in English. In heated French I told him to shut up and stop playing the bloody fool, walked away and made sure that I was nowhere near him when we set off again. Not long afterwards Rafferty was picked up in Clermont-Ferrand because, it was reported, he had been too casual about a conversation (this time in French) in a café. One report said he had been heard to say he was looking forward to a moonlight operation. Whatever the reason was, Rafferty paid with his life. He spent two years in concentration camps before being shot a couple of months before the war ended.

Being a secret agent could be terribly boring at times. You might spend six weeks hanging about, trying to be inconspicuous, just for the sake of an hour's work which, if it went according to plan, was not very exciting in any case. You had to be on the right spot at the right time, available and in contact with your superiors up to the moment of action. In between times there was the simple question to be faced of making yourself scarce. You had to eat somewhere, sleep somewhere and occasionally you felt a desperate need to talk to someone, even though you were aware that to do so could be dangerous, if not fatal. Boredom was, in fact, a menace that no one was taught to contend with at the training school. Boredom was something individuals had to deal with themselves, and it cost quite a few men and women their lives when they came up with the wrong solution.

The most insidious thing about it was that it induced a sense of security at just the moment when one should have been alert for surprise moves by the enemy. I learned this to my cost during a gloriously sunny spell in Paris in June 1943.

Having contacted Lejeune I was obliged to wait for a courier to pass on a message to Lyons that I would be somewhat later in returning than I had anticipated – there were some minor snags I had to iron out – and that meant kicking my heels for a while.

It was strange and irritating being an outcast in the place of my birth, a Paris that was far from what I was used to, a city almost deserted. For a start there was hardly any traffic. If you saw a petrol-driven car it contained either Germans, or collaborators, or some essential user like a doctor. The ordinary Frenchmen chugged about the boulevards from time to time in weird contraptions with small furnaces at the rear which supplied wood gas to a balloon-like container on the roof. The top-speed of these *gazogènes* was claimed to be about 30 m.p.h. going downhill with the wind behind them, but even that was an exaggeration. Anyway, the appearance of even these monstrosities was rare and it was possible to cross the road to the Arc de Triomphe in complete safety. If you were going to be knocked down by anything it was more likely to be a cyclist or a *vélo taxi*. The latter was a primitive substitute for the ordinary cab and consisted of a hefty two-wheel bicycle towing a wickerwork seat for two people. There was no shortage of fares for them, as long as it wasn't raining, and it was quite customary for couples to make their way even to night-clubs in the *velos*. The *velo* drivers developed leg-muscles as hard as billiard balls. A man has to be pretty fit to cycle all the way up the Champs Elysees towing, perhaps, twenty stone behind him.

Gone with the peace-time traffic jams were the crowds. The café tables which would have been packed on a normal summer's day had a forlorn look about them. If they boasted more than a handful of people it was wise to avoid them; almost certainly they were patronized by Germans or their sympathizers. But rationing was the main cause for the empty tables. The French who could afford to spend their money on black market food took it home to cook. They could see no point in allowing a restaurateur to add his charges to the already exorbitant price of food and vegetables.

I confined myself to eating only once or twice a week in a black-market restaurant even though I had no problem with money. It was just a question of not drawing attention to yourself. Big restaurants were places to be avoided. So were hotels. The Gestapo, and indeed the French police, had a nasty habit of inspecting registers in the early hours of the morning. To a knock on the door an Englishman dreaming of home might easily reply in his own language 'Yes?' or 'Who is it?' That was not all. If they didn't like your writing, or if you had an unusual name, you heard a knock on your bedroom door at 6 a.m. and had to answer a lot of questions about what you were doing in Paris and who your friends were. A visit to the local police station followed if you were unable to answer the questions satisfactorily.

Much safer places to spend an undisturbed night were the *maisons de passe*. One thing the Germans had not closed down were the brothels and they put the *maisons de passe* more or less on the same level. These were generally crumbling, rather scruffy hotels where a man could take girl for a couple of hours at any time of the day or night with no questions asked. It was an old French custom and to have instituted systematic searches would have been very impractical, as there were literally hundreds of these establishments. Furthermore, there was no question of the owners of the *maisons de passe* asking his visitors to sign in. And so you were safe, or as safe as anything could be for an agent. You could book a room, say you were expecting mademoiselle, and as there was a constant flow of females no one had any reason to disbelieve you, and put up your feet for a few hours.

To travel about the city was to ask for trouble, especially if one had lived there. One evening on my way to meet Delphin I was travelling on the Metro when I noticed a plump, dark girl whom I recognized immediately as a member of a family who had been friends of my own people for years. I had not seen Madeleine since 1939 but it was quite clear that she had also recognized me. It was equally clear that she had no intention of saying or doing anything unless I indicated that it was all right. When the compartment began to empty I was able to join her and, while we rattled along, I asked politely about her parents and about her brothers and sisters, just as if I had bumped into a neighbour I had not seen for some time, which was, I suppose true. In turn she discreetly confined herself to harmless chatter about the topics of the day, although she must have been baffled to know what an Englishman was doing in the heart of Occupied France. As if it were the most normal thing in the world, she invited me home to dine with her mother and father. Gracefully, I accepted, fully aware that I had to make quite sure that neither the girl nor her family would breathe a word to their friends about my unexpected appearance.

What followed at Madeleine's home in the Passy district turned out to be a complicated charade.

'Look who is here, Maman.'

An elderly French woman turned from her task at the kitchen table where she was busy with a vegetable knife and gave a little gasp. Slowly she walked towards me, still clutching the knife, then circled me once and yet again before she threw her arms about me and wept on my shoulder. I stood there smiling self-consciously and gave her a reassuring squeeze.

'Jean has come to supper, mother,' said her daughter brightly. 'I met him on the Metro. Don't you think you ought to tell Papa.'

But Papa, who appeared without his collar or jacket, was already putting his head round the door.

His eyes were round with amazement.

'Jean!' he exclaimed. 'What on earth are you doing here.'

'Don't be silly, Papa,' said his wife sniffing back her tears, 'can't you see he has come to supper. Aren't you going to offer him a glass of wine?'

The kitchen knife which she was still grasping was waved in the direction of the large old-fashioned sideboard.

'But, of course,' he replied, recovering his composure and wringing my hand. 'But, of course.'

And so we dined – Papa having restored his collar and jacket for the occasion and Mama having divested herself of her apron.

'And how is your father?'

'In splendid health.'

'And have you seen Monsieur and Madame So-and-so?', a reference to some other family friends in Paris.

'I am afraid that I have not had the time.'

'But, naturally, you are busy?'

'Yes maman. There is much to do these days.'

Gradually, without revealing a single fact, a rapport was established which reassured me that I had nothing to fear.

Whether they guessed that I was an agent I do not know, but that I was working against the Germans and needed their silence they had no doubt.

Papa walked as far as the Metro with me when I left.

'You know you can count on us if you need anything,' he said as we shook hands. 'Only be careful.'

This encounter with the family in Passy cheered me up considerably. In that suburban house I had met the French I really admired, devoted to their family and to their friends. After I left the Metro and walked through the night, the familiar buildings seemed to offer their very shadows as allies. Even the greasy-haired patron of the *maison de passe* seemed to put a little warmth into his leer as I checked in.

The following morning, possibly influenced by the nostalgia conjured up the previous night, I decided to call on another old friend of the family. Jim Pratt had known my father since they were young men when both had been leading lights in the flourishing English sporting fraternity which dominated racing and boxing in Paris at the turn of the century. Jim was among the first of the big promoters to realize the potential of staging big fights in France and he brought over such champions as Jack Johnson. He became official time-keeper for all the top matches and in the end assumed French nationality. Despite his success in the world of boxing, Jim still remained fond of racing and kept a stable at Neuilly long after my father left France. It was to this yard that I made my way on the afternoon after my trip to Passy. I would have gone earlier in the day but knowing Jim's rather frugal ways – he didn't believe in giving anything away if he could avoid it – I had lunch in a small restaurant, using a ration coupon, and then set off.

The old man was not at home, I was told when I first inquired, but I eventually tracked him down by heading in the direction of a string of curses coming from a small yard at the back of his house. There I saw the familiar, burly six-foot-four-inch figure of the old gentleman, who was then in his eighties, performing gyrations that would have defied many a younger man as he tried to overcome the objections of a wild-eyed mare to accepting the attentions of an equally excited stallion.

A diminutive French stable lad was rolling on the ground while Jim held the mare's snorting head. To Jim my appearance was neither a surprise nor a matter for comment: it was the Lord's answer to a prayer that he considered was undoubtedly his due.

'Don't just stand there,' he bellowed in French. 'Get the shackles on her.'

At the end of a dusty half-hour the mare's hind legs were well and truly shackled and an almost frenzied stallion performed his duties in such an energetic way that all the rebellion was knocked out of the fractious female. Only when the horses were eventually led to their boxes did Jim find time for a chat. The conversation was restricted solely to horses and the effect the accursed war had had on racing. I don't think Jim gave a thought to the fact that it was highly unusual, to say the least, for an English visitor to drop in on him. He had been part of the international scene for so long he didn't take boundaries and squabbles between countries seriously. To him I was a sportsman. I was also a Parisian. He had known me since I was a baby, and my arrival that afternoon had been most opportune and natural. He didn't ask what I was doing in Paris and I didn't tell him. After sharing a glass of wine he sent me on my way with: 'Give my regards to your father.'

I told him I would, although I had no idea when I would see him again.

My bout of stud work left me in a cheerful frame of mind and I could discern only one cloud on the horizon the following morning in that it was a *jour sans*, one of the loathesome non-alcoholic days. Every other day was a *jour sans*, in order, it was said, to conserve the country's wine stocks, although it was obvious that the liquor saved was going to fill German bellies. For the Boche every day was a *jour avec*. Even the collaborators resented it. To loyal Frenchmen it was infuriating.

The Nazi bureaucrats inflicted many humiliations and indignities on Occupied France but this was one of the most stupid. Wine is part of a Frenchman's soul. It is indispensable. It is sacred. During the darkest days of Verdun in 1916, the ration carriers, usually the worst shots in a regiment, risked their lives to bring flasks of rough red *pinard* to their comrades in the cratered fields. Only the dull, humourless Master Race could have been so insensitive to a national characteristic as to invite the further wrath of an oppressed people. The only consolation to people like myself was the comforting thought that in such uncivilized circumstances no self-respecting Frenchman could possibly co-operate with the invaders.

The *jour sans* had its dangers as well as its irritations. More than one agent, newly-arrived from England, gave himself away by ordering *vermouth cassis* on the wrong day. And there were plenty of informers hanging about ready to run to the Gestapo to report that a gentleman was ordering *vermouth cassis* when law-abiding citizens should be sticking to soft drinks.

That was one mistake I did not intend to make as I headed down the Champs Elysées to meet the courier who was to take my message to Lyons at eight o'clock that night. In a narrow side street I found the bar I was looking for. It was the sort of little den known in those days as a Pam Pam. Paris had scores of them and they were ideal for clandestine meetings because you could select a different one each time.

I took my seat at one end of the long, mahogany counter which ran the length of one side of the room, from where, perched insecurely on a ricketty cane chair I was able to view the rest of the room in the mirror half-hidden behind shelves covered with a variety of bottles, nearly all of which were empty. A tariff of *consommations* struck a reproachful note, with its boast of unobtainable champagne. The wall behind me had no doubt been a fashionable green and gold flower design in the Naughty Nineties but it had since adopted a more retiring attitude and skulked dully under a brown patina of either dirt or varnish or both. Some philistine has further offended the walls by hammering in two large nails, from one of which hung a calendar for the previous year while the other bore a notice concerning the curfew. The black letters, printed on antiseptically white paper, scowled down on half a dozen shiny red and white oil cloths gracing a row of humble tables with iron ball and claw feet.

The customers were as unspectacular as their surroundings. A slightly-built man in blue overalls leaned against the bar just inside the door as if he realized that his stained brown rubber boots were unwelcome. From the conversation I gathered he worked for a horse slaughterer and was the uncle of the sallow boy who had served my orange juice and was now leisurely polishing a glass. They carried on a non-stop conversation with two locals sitting in their shirt sleeves who faced each other across a table but constantly looked over their shoulders to shout leg-pulling remarks in the Paris argot. They went unnoticed by a young couple who sat sharing the same glass of Diabolo Menthe, taking alternate sips The bright-faced girl splashed some on her white blouse and giggled as the boy tried to rub out the bright green mark. A motherly woman, with a florid face and untidy blonde hair piled up on her head, appeared from behind the curtains in the corner and offered a clean cloth. A strong smell of garlic floated in with her and from her manner it was obvious that she was the owner and young sallow-face was her son.

A more disapproving glance at the lovers was given by a square old woman in an incongruously flowered hat. Beside her sat an old gentleman with a face of one of the heroes of the Marne, staring blankly over a walrus moustache, his huge red hands clamped over the handle of a walking-stick which he held upright between his knees. A large basket stood on the seat beside the woman. They must have been country folk returning from a visit to relatives. Their basket was empty, but they looked as though they fed well enough.

I glanced at the faces. No one looked oppressed. There was no immediate evidence that anyone was suffering any form of hardship. Did they really know there was a war on? Did the fashionable ladies and gentlemen you saw in the street being pedalled off to their night-clubs realize that young men of their own city were being dragged off every day to indulge in a different form of sweated labour for the Third Reich? Did the young lovers or the old peasants ever read the sinister black and red notices pasted on the walls most mornings announcing the execution of 'communists' and 'terrorists'? Or was it all a dream?

Alone in that little bar, mulling over the quiet family at Passy who had never said a word about the war, thinking of old Jim Pratt who was more concerned with his horses, it was possible to believe that the war was a fantasy.

There was a movement at the door. I glanced at the large station-style clock high on one of the pillars of the bar, solemnly correct despite the dirt which had collected behind its glass. Five minutes to eight. Perhaps this was Pierre, the stolid, fair young railwayman whom I was expecting. Instead an anxious little man clutching a briefcase hurried in, his brim-up-all-the-way-round trilby squarely on his face, spoke to the barman, shook hands with both the locals and the workman, and pushed quickly past me with a nod and ducked behind the counter and vanished. Obviously Madame's husband had to go out to work to keep the place.

At eight o'clock sharp, I glanced at the clock again and then at the door through which I saw a car pull up on the other side of the narrow street. I remember thinking that nothing could get past in either direction until it moved. Four men got out and walked across the cobbles. Without hurrying two took up positions inside the bar, one on each side of the door. The other two kept on walking. There was no mistaking what they were. The cut of their suits, the big-padded shoulders, the drape lapels, the light summer hats, their very walk gave them away.

The banter between the locals stopped dead. The little barman shrank still further into his grimy outsize jacket and stopped polishing. Madame, fussing over the girl's blouse, raised the cloth to her face as if to hide behind it. A flush spread over the young man's face and he leaned over and gripped his sweetheart's wrist. The silence set off some sixth sense alarm in the living-room of the master of the house for his nervous countenance appeared suddenly from between the curtains where it remained, blinking. Only the hero of the Marne remained impassive.

My own first thought was purely sympathetic: 'Some poor beggar's for it now.'

In the mirror I watched the eyes of the other customers follow the intruders. Suddenly the girl was staring straight at me with an expression of shock and terror. Then she was blotted out by the reflections of two of the newcomers and a blow in the ribs sent me reeling from my seat. Another couple of jabs and my back was pressed hard against the counter, my arms were knocked up, and expert hands were searching along my sleeves and legs.

'Gestapo,' said one man curtly in French with a strong German accent. 'You are coming with us.'

Even then I couldn't believe I had been caught. For a moment I believed it was all a joke. But then I felt a feeling that I had never experienced before and have never experienced since. It was not fear. It was a mixture of incredulousness, numbness, shock, of a tremendous racing of the brain trying to comprehend and cope with the situation. The impossible had happened. I had been taken completely by surprise.

I caught a glimpse of myself in the mirror as I was bundled towards the door and was amazed to see that I looked comparatively unruffled. I have no idea how the other customers reacted to my arrest. If they had stood on their hands and sung 'God Save the King' I don't think I would have noticed.

The dominant thought in my head was that 'they', the dreaded, anonymous 'they' had got me. It was no joke after all. That blow in the ribs had come from a very real Schmeisser automatic machine pistol (rather like a British Sten gun), and if I tried to run for it I would be shot down. Not that there was any chance of running for it, as there was only one way in and out of the Pam Pam and the Gestapo toughs were on each side of it. I made a belated note to avoid bars with only one door in future. If there was going to be any future.

Then I seemed to become two Goldsmiths. Goldsmith No. 1, still smartly dressed in his expensive tweed jacket which now bore a tiny smear of oil from the muzzle of the Schmeisser, was scurrying meekly through the narrow door with its guard of honour, followed by a tough with a gun who bore a remarkable resemblance to a bookmaker I used to know. Goldsmith No. 2 stood back watching, straining his eyes for a chance to get away, the opportunity to snatch at the Schmeisser or ... or something.

Goldsmith No. 1 stood by while the driver took over the wheel of the car and one of the men who had guarded the door got in the back seat on the far side.

'This could be the chance,' muttered Goldsmith No. 2, considering a desperate backward fling at the armed captor.

Goldsmith No. 1 reflected that it was unlikely that the rest of the escort were unarmed; and who knew what guns they had in the car? He would wait.

The man on the inside pushed open the door and I got in. The leather smelled slightly of scent, more of cigarettes and strongly of sweat. There was even more perspiration in a minute when the third member of our party pushed himself alongside me in the back seat. Whoever designed that car had certainly never intended that the back seat should carry three men and the two I had to share it with obviously considered that as a newcomer to the scene I had no territorial rights in the matter.

Goldsmith No. 2 winced as he watched No. 1 trying to cram his slim British bottom between two fleshy Boche backsides. Gradually, as my nerves realigned themselves and I squeezed on to the three inches of seat available, the two Goldsmiths got together and decided that in view of the circumstances it was better to postpone any attempt to escape. To start with, the man with the gun had got in alongside the driver and half-turned to face me with the barrel pointing in my direction. Had I tried to leap out he would not have needed to shoot. Either of the thugs could have pulled me back with one hand. As the car roared off at high speed past the deserted cafés I decided that the only thing to do was to play for time. At some juncture I would get a break. It might be just a split second opportunity but I would have to be ready for it. In the meantime ... keep quiet ... keep watching. In particular, keep watching where they are taking you, I told myself.

My first guess was the notorious block 82–86 Avenue Foch, the main counter-espionage headquarters of the Gestapo, to the west of the Arc de Triomphe, and not far from where I had been captured. Everyone in Paris had heard ugly stories about the Avenue Foch and I knew for certain that they were true. Nevertheless when we took a different direction I had slight misgivings. What if I were taken direct either to the Cherche Midi or to Fresnes? That was the last thing I wanted. For both were proper gaols, where I would be put into a proper cell, to rot between the periods of questioning which would undoubtedly take place in one of the Gestapo headquarters. An escape from either of these grim buildings was almost unheard of. Men who disappeared inside there were subject to the pitiless Nacht-und-Nebel Decree of 1941.

This had been issued by Keitel at Hitler's orders after the initial French Resistance attacks on German soldiers. The first reactions of the Germans had been to try suspects by a military court. But the resultant publicity was deemed to do more harm than good by creating the movement's first martyrs. Under the new decree, which literally translated means 'Night and Fog', prisoners were clapped into French gaols and, after interrogation, were spirited away across the border to Germany and were never heard of again, unless they were traced when the concentration camps were over-run at the end of the war.

At Fresnes and Cherche Midi, where they were held, it was not unusual for a man to be manacled for months at a time in solitary confinement. To make the possibility of escape even more difficult their gaolers were French '*milice*', locally recruited auxiliaries of the Gestapo who frequently outdid their mentors in brutality. Speaking the same language, knowing the questions to ask, they were much more dangerous to an agent than a German.

While these thoughts went through my head, our car, a big black Citroën, raced through the streets. What cars we encountered got out of our way. The black Citroën was the hall mark of the Gestapo and everyone knew it. Fast and reliable, it was the first of the big front-wheel-drive cars – *traction avant* – and could corner very tightly. The Germans preferred it even to their own Mercedes.

Our particular vehicle had little to recommend it as far as I was concerned until it pulled up with a jerk in the Place des États-Unis. My fellow travellers, who had not spoken a word to me since my arrest, indicated that I should get out. The man with the gun, who was obviously in charge, led the way into what appeared to be a large block of flats. At least, I thought, it is not the Cherche Midi or Fresnes.

A couple of brawny civilians glanced up momentarily as we entered the hall but took no particular notice. A flight of stairs led to the first floor where a door was opened and I was led into what could have been a small apartment.

A plain wooden table stood in the middle of the room under an electric light with a nondescript shade. About a dozen chairs were scattered about the carpeted room. The German in charge pointed to a chair by the table and told me to sit down. I obeyed promptly. His comrades then distributed themselves around the room and relaxed. They still said nothing to me although occasionally they would pass monosyllabic remarks in German. This left me completely in the dark for although I am bilingual, this is purely an accident through my having been brought up in France and not due to any aptitude for languages. My gaolers regarded me with an air of utter indifference. I felt that perhaps they were disappointed in me. Perhaps they would have preferred me to give them a run for my money, a struggle or a shout. They were obviously bored with the whole affair, giving the impression that they had been on duty all day and now they would like to retire for the night. When one of them lit a cigarette I asked if I might smoke too. The man with the gun had no objection.

I lit a Gauloise and tried to appear what I can only describe as neutral. Don't upset anyone, I kept on telling myself. I made sure that I did not even catch the eyes of my guards. I did not want them to think I was cocky or trying to take the mickey or putting on a bold front. I didn't want to provoke anyone or anything. I did not know how they were going to play it but I would find out soon enough. Suddenly I realized that I wanted like mad to relieve my bursting bladder.

'Can I use the lavabo?'

'It's over there,' said the No. 1 man, pointing to a door.

'Use it but leave the door open.'

I stood over the lavatory pan for what seemed a lifetime, my mind stimulated by the sight of the big bath in the same room. My eyes searched anxiously for any sign of a wooden rod. One did not have to find signs of bloodstains to confirm that an otherwise innocent room had been used as a torture chamber. The latest methods I had heard about obviated any such unseemliness. All that happened was that a bath was filled and the prisoner, bound hand and foot, balanced like a trussed chicken on a bar of wood. If he did not answer the questions put to him a slight push sent him face forward into the water. At the point of drowning he was pulled out and balanced again. Another question, the wrong answer, and a gentle tap on the head sent the dripping, gasping individual plunging into the water once again. All reports said that the results of this torture had been most effective, at least as far as the Gestapo were concerned.

Back in the room, I noticed that there was a telephone. But it was the directory on which my eye fastened with trepidation. The Paris directory, the Bottin, unlike our London directory is not split up into so many sections but published in one great tome about a foot high. This particular one had an extremely dirty cover as if someone had wiped his feet on it and I remembered another unpleasant habit of the Gestapo. A prisoner, with arms bound, is perched on the directory. As he tries to keep his balance on this small platform his captors use him as a punchbag. The feeling of helplessness induced by such treatment was said to be heartbreaking – and nerve-breaking. The Bottin did not appeal to me at all.

I concentrated on keeping my thoughts on other things. On who had betrayed me, for example. Gradually I came to the unhappy conclusion that it could only be my courier. No other person knew of our rendezvous. Delphin certainly did not know it and I had been in Paris too short a time for anyone else in the Resistance to make contact. Jim Pratt I ruled out right away; and how could Madeleine and her parents in Passy have possibly known that I was going to a bar off the Étoile? No, the finger pointed at Pierre. Like me he was a Parisian by birth although, also like me, his family were foreigners, in his case from Russia.

I wondered what folly had persuaded him to turn traitor. Was it the temptation of the German offer of a million francs for anyone who helped in the capture of a British officer? Did he need the money for a girl? To gamble? To set up a business?

I wracked my brains to think of any other contacts of mine that he might denounce, and I thanked heaven that I had trusted him only with simple messages. I wondered what was going on behind his striking blue eyes at that very moment. Was he frightened too? For he must have known that if ever it leaked out that he was a traitor, his life was worth about as much to the Resistance's specially-trained teams of killers as mine was to the Gestapo.

If he needed anything at that moment, it was the news that I was dead or doomed. Should I make contact with the outside world he was beyond help.

An hour passed while I sat there very, very busy with my own musing, offending no one, doing nothing except smoke. Before the war, as a keep-fit fanatic I had smoked, at the most, three cigarettes a day. During the war my consumption rose to fifty a day and has remained there ever since.

The Germans smoked too, and one of them tidily emptied my ashtray when it looked like overflowing. Still only the odd word was spoken, still they did not show their hand. They had got the art of sagging at the alert down to a fine art. Then the door swung open and they stiffened to attention, assuming wooden but expectant expressions. A plump figure, in a well-pressed brown light-weight suit strode confidently into the room. His pink, clean-shaven face wore an air of slight amusement.

Glancing quickly around the room his eyes eventually fell upon me, still sitting, still smoking, still sticking to my doctrine of neutrality. A pause, and then he deigned to notice me.

'I'm sorry I kept you waiting so long,' he said in faultless French. 'I'm afraid I was having dinner when I was informed of your arrival.'

As I could think of nothing to say I remained quiet.

My interrogator patted his pink silk breast-pocket handkerchief thoughtfully, cocked his head on one side and then motioned to one of his minions. A chair was drawn towards the other side of the table, perhaps two feet or so from it, and my visitor took his seat, carefully hitching up his trousers. His attitude was that of a top-class tycoon who is about to employ a clerk at £8 a week and finds the whole business rather distasteful.

For some time no further remarks were made, but it was obvious that the actors were taking their places for their parts in an old routine. I kept my eyes on the floor. Two pairs of large feet appeared on each side of my chair. I recognized the shoes. They belonged to my possessive friends from the back seat of the Citroën. One of them, a red-haired giant, took his position slightly to the right and behind me. The other stood on my left. This time I had the seat all to myself. Elsewhere in the room I could sense the other Germans taking up familiar positions.

'I know you are an officer and a British officer.'

The words were spoken quietly, almost confidentially. There was no menace in them. Just a plain statement of fact.

'What is your rank?'

'I am not a British officer. I am a Frenchman. I come from Paris and my papers will tell you all about me.'

I might as well have spoken to the moon. He took no notice.

'It is useless to lie,' the calm, polite voice continued. 'You may as well tell me your rank. You see I know all about you.'

Did he, by jove! He sounded so sure that I was beginning to wonder just how much he did know. Still, I had a cover story and I was going to stick to it.

'My name is Jean Delannoy, I'm a Parisian and I do not know what you are talking about.'

'All right, let me see your papers.'

I handed them across the table and one of my guards passed them to the man in brown. Carefully he went through them, all the time probing quietly with questions. Every so often he would shake his head slightly. If he noticed those of my papers which were forged he did not say so. He merely discarded them.

'These are useless,' he said. 'I have told you I know who you are.'

My prized *affiche*, the one genuine document in my possession, a railway pass which enabled me to travel over a large area of France, received the same scornful treatment.

'Tell me again who you say you are,' he asked, pursing his lips and folding his hands, fingers entwined on his lap.

For about the fourth time I went into my well-rehearsed cover story.

I was Jean Delannoy, I was a dealer, a general dealer, and I admitted I did a bit on the side for the black market. As for my background, it was simple.

Telling the tale of Jean Delannoy's life was not difficult. It was exactly the same as my own, up to a point. That was what had been arranged in England months before. If ever I were questioned I would stick to the details of my own early life as closely as possible. I would use slang that only a native-born Parisian could know, *falzar* for trousers, *godasse* for shoes, etc., to convince any questioners that indeed I had been to school in the area of the

Avenue du Bois de Boulogne – now ironically renamed the Avenue Foch. After all it was true. I had started my scholastic career at the College Janson de Sailly in the Rue de Longchamp and had gradually worked my way down through four other schools by steadfastly refusing to go to Mass on Thursdays on the grounds that I was a Protestant.

The Man in Brown was not impressed by my local knowledge. Weaknesses in my cover story now began to become painfully apparent.

One of the greatest difficulties was that I had left the area when I was only 17, some fifteen years previously. Furthermore, in order to avoid being conscripted for forced labour in Germany I had added a few years to my age. If the Gestapo cared to check, and it would not take them long, they would soon find questions that I could not answer.

'So you were born in the Rue de la Faisanderie, off the Boulevard Lannes?'

'Yes.' That at least was true.

'What was your father's job?'

'Well, he was always interested in horses. He did a little trading.' That was also true. But he had left Paris long before the war and so had I.

'You realize that all I have to do is to send down to the Rue de la Faisanderie and I can check on this?'

There was no doubt about that. A quick trip in the black Citroën back to the street of my birth would not reveal my father's yard which had vanished long ago, but there would be people who remembered an English family who used to live there. There would be nobody to remember Jean Delannoy.

I said nothing.

Without any warning a tremendous, stinging blow sent me lurching against the table and I retched and gasped as I clung to it, choking on my cigarette smoke.

The red-headed giant sniffed and pulled his jacket down over his striped shirt cuffs.

I waited dazed for the next punch from his hairy hands but it did not come. I sat upright again and tried to pretend that it had been of no consequence, that it hadn't hurt. Deliberately I pushed the cigarette into the ashtray.

The Man in Brown showed no sign of emotion at all.

'Come along, I know this is your cover story. A child could see through it. Now tell me your rank.'

I rambled on about being Delannoy at the same time waiting to catch the next blow on my elbow and shield my head. Nothing happened.

'It is no good. I really do know all about you. Didn't you realize that we had you tailed all yesterday?'

This might or might not have been true.

'You went to Neuilly, didn't you?'

'Nonsense I never left . . .' another almighty blow from Red Hair caught me completely by surprise. Once again I had to cling to the table to prevent myself sprawling on the floor. More than anything I felt I wanted to show that the punch had not really hurt me. Don't ask me why. I don't know. I just didn't want them to have that particular pleasure.

I suppose I was struck about half a dozen times in all. Red Hair was a past master at the art of inflicting unexpected and crude pain. Never once did I manage to anticipate his move. Had I done so I might not now be slightly deaf in my right ear.

Throughout this part of the interrogation, the Man in Brown remained unruffled and almost courteous.

As if to emphasize the superiority of his position he announced that he was head of the Paris Gestapo. That gave me further food for thought. If that were true, then he was Müller, a tough and clever officer. A nagging thought began to creep in that he just might know all about me. Then, in a careless moment, he made a tiny slip.

'Why don't you just admit it,' he said, 'you were parachuted into France to spy on us? You see, we know . . .'

The sight of a chink in the armour of this apparently impervious brute gave fresh strength to my flagging hopes and soothed my aching head.

Müller did not know everything after all. Müller did not know all about me. Müller was lying. Müller was guessing. I had landed by Lizzie – that remarkable light aircraft, the Lysander.

Another thought struck me. Pierre, pitiful Pierre, had also been under the impression that I had been parachuted into the country and I had not seen any reason to disillusion him. The finger was beginning to point very firmly in the direction of the traitor.

It was ironic that the man who had betrayed me had become the means of giving me an opportunity to weigh up my opponent. Müller, I came to the conclusion, was not the genius he thought himself to be. So I would try a new line. I would pander to his vanity. If we could spin out the proceedings, I might gain the time I needed.

'Look,' I said leaning over the table confidentially, 'you have said that you are head of the Gestapo in Paris. Well, it has been clear to me ever since you came into the room that you are an officer despite your civilian clothes. Is that not correct?'

Müller saw little harm in humouring me.

'What if it is?' he replied.

'Well, although I am in plain clothes, it is apparently obvious to you that I am an officer also.'

'So?'

'Ah! Just imagine for a moment that our positions are reversed and that I am interrogating you. Would you, a German officer and gentleman, betray your friends?'

I remained leaning across the table, my eyes fixed on his.

'Well, would you? Even if he (and here I nodded to Red Hair still poised ominously at my side) were doing his strong arm act?'

For the first time that evening, Müller showed a slight sign of surprise. He blinked a couple of times. If I had called him a swine, or a rat or a butcher, I do not think he would have turned a hair. I have no doubt that he was used to standing unmoved while tortured wretches damned him with their dying breath. But to be called a gentleman!

Somewhere at the back of his nasty little Nazi mind there lurked, perhaps, an inbred Germanic longing to be a member of the ancient Prussian ruling class.

Hitler himself had the same inferiority complex where the Officer Corps was concerned. So did many other top-ranking Party members. Müller was no exception. It was one thing to be feared as a Gestapo boss, but in the end he was still only a glorified policeman. Officers were different.

He rubbed his hands thoughtfully on his plump thighs, as if polishing his well-creased trousers, while he debated with himself

the question of whether he would confess in the unlikely event of
being knocked about by one of his own thugs. Finally, almost as if
taken aback by his own words, he spoke.

'No,' he said, 'I do not think I would.'

I felt the atmosphere in the room change. A new caste system
had been established. Psychologically Müller and I were on a
different and higher plane from the crude dolts under his orders.
We were gentlemen, belonging to a fraternity they couldn't hope
to join. No longer did I feel an underdog to be kicked around by
all and sundry. I felt, subtly, that for a brief moment I had the
initiative.

'You say that you wouldn't betray your friends in these circumstances,' I repeated pressing home the point.

'No.'

'Then why ask me to?'

Müller smiled a bland smile and kept on rubbing his thighs. The
situation appealed to him. He could show off to his men. He could
indulge in generous gestures. He could make me feel humiliated
and grateful to him. And all the time he could savour the sadistic
pleasure of knowing that I was completely at his mercy.

I waited.

'All right,' he said. 'I salute you as a British Officer and a gentleman. And, for tonight, I will treat you as one. For this night only.
But let me warn you. Although you are a brave man, tomorrow
you will tell me all I want to know. Or if not tomorrow the next
day. I have the means and the men to make you talk.'

'And remember, we are in no hurry. We have all the time in the
world. As you know everyone talks in the end. You can save yourself a lot of trouble if you make up your mind soon enough.'

Müller knew what he was saying. Nearly everyone talked under
torture in the end. If they didn't, it was generally due to an excess
of enthusiasm on the part of their tormentors who allowed death
to intervene too soon. I wondered just how long I could go without cracking ... twenty-four hours, a week, six weeks. It was
something that could only be learned by experience. I thought of
the French officer who had leaped to his death from the third floor
window of the Gestapo headquarters at Lyons. A brave man.
Would I have the guts to do the same?

While these thoughts ran through my mind, Müller carried on

with his quiet coaxing. Then his eyes lit with inspiration.

'Do you like champagne?' he asked in a jolly tone.

The question took me completely by surprise. Ridiculously I wanted to say: 'But it is a *jour sans*.' Instead I nodded assent.

'Then we shall split a bottle.'

With a jerk of his head he summoned one of his minions and spoke rapidly in German. The man, the one who looked like a bookmaker, glanced at me briefly and left the room. I remained seated, feeling distinctly uncomfortable.

There was something very unreal about the situation. A warning which had been given to us at one of the S.O.E. schools came back to me uneasily. Most people had heard of the old trick of using two interrogators, Herr Nasty and Herr Nice. The first was used to bully and ill-treat the prisoner, shouted, used his fists and threatened. After a period of brutality he would leave the room and in would come his charming friend, a quiet understanding man who would perhaps offer the prisoner a cup of coffee and a cigarette, who would assure him that he wanted to help him, to spare him further pain and indignity. All he had to do was confide in Herr Nice and he could see that no further unpleasantness took place.

Only the most naïve prisoners were taken in by this old trick and the Gestapo knew it. So they introduced a refinement for tougher opponents. After Herr Nasty had done his stuff they would bring in Herr Nice to deliver his usual soft soap. At the end of it he would give his victim a cigarette and ask him if he would like a cup of coffee. When the coffee arrived he would hold the cup in his hand, talking as pleasantly as ever, until the prisoner began to think he would never get it. Finally he would hand it over, and as the prisoner raised it to his grateful lips, Herr Nice would hit him with all his force, sending cup and cigarette flying. This sudden and unexpected reversal of tactics had been known to reduce strong men to tears and I wondered if the champagne ploy was in a similar vein.

Whether the champagne came from some sort of mess in the building or whether it came from Müller's private stocks I do not know, but it arrived within a matter of minutes. There were only two glasses, both crystal champagne goblets. Müller himself did the opening and pouring.

'Good health,' he said sardonically, raising his glass to his lips. '*Salut*,' I replied, raising the glass cautiously to my lips, one eye on Red Hair. Nothing happened. I sipped again then sat back to listen while Müller enjoyed his new game of playing at being a gentleman.

When my glass was empty he refilled it and I waited for the catch while he continued his probing. I ignored the strict S.O.E. order to say nothing at all when captured. Instead I gave the impression of trying to co-operate and told him that I had been sent over to reorganize the Carte Circuit which had been penetrated by the Germans and blown earlier in the year. Müller listened in a bored fashion knowing as well as I did that the only men I had named were now dead.

'You will have to do better than that tomorrow,' he said almost cheerfully. 'I will expect a lot more names, a lot more.'

He talked in a professional way about the Carte organization, how it had operated and how the Germans had infiltrated it long before they started to arrest the members. He gave the impression that there was little he did not know about the espionage circuits in France.

My interrogation had lasted some three hours when, just after midnight, the champagne bottle was emptied and Müller stood up and announced he was leaving.

'My men will take you to your hotel,' he said.

I could hardly believe my ears and raised a quizzical eyebrow.

'Yes, we will put you in an hotel for tonight,' he explained benignly. 'An hotel reserved for officers.'

At the door, he paused and added in a colder tone. 'I will call for you at 10 a.m. Remember what I have said. I have the men and means to make you talk and I shall have no hesitation in using them.' He said something in German to the head of his little squad and, with a nod and a 'Good night' in my direction he left. About five minutes later we all trooped after him, the man with the gun once again covering me. The empty champagne bottle and glasses had the room to themselves.

The journey to the hotel was a short one, our black Citroën pulling up outside the main entrance of the Hotel Continentale in the Rue de Rivoli.

Although it was then about half an hour after midnight, it was still busy with German officers in uniform coming and going. Guards with steel helmets and rifles stood on each side of the door. They looked at me curiously as I was ushered in at the point of the gun.

My escort had been as silent as usual during the journey but their leader now took me over to the reception desk which was manned by an N.C.O. in uniform. A few words in German were exchanged and then I was told:

'Right, sign in.'

The book was pushed towards us.

'What do I sign?' I asked my captor.

'Your right name, of course,' he said.

Without a word I took the pen the clerk was holding out. As I did so my escort craned their necks over my shoulder.

There at the end of a page covered in ugly black script proclaiming the presence of sundry hauptmanns and leutnants I appended the name: Captain John Goldsmith, R.A.C.

The clerk stared at it unbelievingly. My escorts grinned and exchanged nods and winks of Wagnerian proportions. In their eyes I had signed my death warrant.

We now marched in procession through the plush foyer and lounge where various officers sitting in armchairs sipping coffee were informed that I was a captured British spy. The message didn't seem to get home to all of them, however, and from the pointing fingers I gathered that some of my fellow guests had mistaken Red Hair for the villain of the piece – mainly because he towered above everyone, being a good six-foot-six. He showed signs of irritation and, hoping that he would not vent his anger on me, I tried to look more like a spy.

As the lift was not working, the current temporarily switched off to save electricity, we started a long trek up the stairs, now and again encountering residents in uniform who were informed of my identity. On the third floor we turned left down a passage and stopped outside the first door on the right. One of my entourage opened it and Red Hair gave me a push which propelled me inside a smart room with a double bed with a satin coverlet.

'All right,' said the man with the gun, 'let's have your shoe-laces and your braces and tie.'

I did as I was told, reflecting at the same time that it was a somewhat casual way to prevent me committing suicide, for I could easily have fashioned a rope from the bed-sheets and hanged myself had I been so inclined.

As I stood there with my hands in my pockets to hold up my trousers two of my guards looked quickly round the room while a third disappeared only to return a few minutes later. Through the half open door I saw the uniform of a Wehrmacht soldier whom I gathered was being stationed in the corridor. There was some conversation among the Gestapo men and then they left.

'We will be back to collect you at ten o'clock,' said their leader menacingly. '*Wiedersehn!*' Then he shut the door behind him, and turned the key. Outside I heard a chair scrape as the sentry settled himself for the night. It was time to be frightened.

I had never given much thought to God before that night. In my view most people don't unless they are in a tight corner. But if there was a God, I told myself, then he would prove it by getting me out of this. In the meantime, I would do all in my power to assist Him in the operation. Every instinct told me that if I were to escape, it would have to be from that room – and within a matter of hours.

That room. It was packed with things that were patently useless to a would-be runaway. What good was a dressing-table to me? I could be a cringing cripple within twenty-four hours and yet the dressing-table would still be there, unfeeling and unscarred, reflecting the face of some square-headed German officer. The wardrobe with its two coathangers, the chairs, the wastepaper basket became objects of hatred and frustration because of their inanimate neutrality.

I prowled round like a bag fox in a stable the night before a hunt. The walls, the floor and the ceiling all received my concentrated attention in case they should reveal a flaw I could exploit. The builders of the Hotel Continentale must have served their apprenticeship on Norman Castles, I decided; the structure seemed to be solid through and through. Switching off the light I drew back the blackout curtain and gently tried the catch of the window. It refused to budge. I applied further pressure until it creaked open. I swallowed hard and glowered into the night.

The hotel was built around a large courtyard. This had been

glazed in at the level of the first floor to provide a winter garden and the glass roof shone in the bright moonlight. Even if I had been able to lower myself on ropes made from the bed linen, I could never have got past this obstacle except by crashing through it. I studied the pronounced shadows on the other side of the rectangle. After a time I became aware that the hotel must have been added to at different periods. In the block opposite, for example, every window had its own sill. The side of the rectangle immediately adjacent to the part of the building where I was imprisoned was different. An ornamental frieze ran the length of it and served as a sill for all the windows. About eighteen inches wide and slightly sloping to drain off rainwater, this ledge ran round the inside corner of the hotel to serve as a sill for the window of my own room. I stared at it longingly. In the shadows there was no way of knowing whether or not the ledge was broken but it seemed obvious that this was the way I would have to go. Past the corner I could see an open window through which I could re-enter the hotel. A pale glow came from inside the room, but I decided to postpone the problem of dispatching any slumbering Germans I might encounter until the situation arose.

At this point a call of nature, induced by nervousness as much as by the champagne, led me to visit the splendid bathroom which formed part of my accommodation. I was thoughtfully fastening my fly-buttons when the answer to my prayers was revealed to me. High up on the wall, above the lavatory, I noticed a narrow, horizontal ventilation window. It was open and was much nearer to the room I hoped to reach than the other window.

I went straight to work – I lowered the lavatory seat; I covered it with the bath mat; I carried in one of the bathroom chairs and placed it carefully on the mat. Hauling myself up by the pipe leading to the cistern, I climbed gingerly into a kneeling position on the chair. It creaked horribly but it held my weight. Slowly I straightened up. I froze as there were more ominous creaks. Still there was no sound of movement from the sentry outside. The thick walls which penned me in also deadened the noise. My chest was now level with the window. I pushed it open gently and stuck my head out.

The scene was peaceful. All was silent. The glass roof of the winter garden glistened like a silver lake. To my left I noticed with some alarm that the ledge finished unexpectedly only a few yards away. The rooms behind that all had separate sills. To the right, thank God, the dark line ran sweet and true to the corner and carried on at right angles to it without a break to the open window.

Delicately withdrawing my head, I put the pane on the catch and lowered myself to the accompaniment of more loud squeaks. As I did so my unfettered trousers descended around my knees.

It was just as well that this scene from a Robertson-Hare farce took place when it did. A similar exhibition at a crucial moment once I was on the ledge could have meant an ignominious end to everything. There and then I attached one of the buttons meant for my braces to my top fly button-hole. Once I felt confident that my trousers would remain in position, I sat down on the bed to consider the timing of my break-out.

My instinct, naturally enough, was to get out as quickly as possible, but cooler consideration made me decide to wait. Assuming that I did achieve my object and reach the streets, I would be abroad between the curfew hours of 11 p.m. and 5 a.m. Although it was possible that a German patrol might give a little leeway to early workmen it was unlikely that they would overlook a man in my dishevelled condition. Furthermore I had no papers or any personal possessions, all of which had been removed at the Place des États-Unis. I determined to wait and lay back watching the darkness change, give way to twilight and the greyness of dawn.

Although I had no means of telling the time, I reckoned that it was four-thirty when once again I creaked my way on to the chair over the lavatory pan. It seemed incredible to me that this noise had gone unheard, and when I began struggling to get my shoulders through the window, bumping against the open pane which hung loose as I could find no way to jam it, it seemed to me that half of Paris must be roused.

I stopped wriggling and remained poised, half in and half out of the room. My problem was to get my head and one shoulder through the window and then swivel on my chest pulling up one leg until I could jam my knee in the corner of the aperture and eventually thrust my foot out. I would then reverse my position swinging my head and shoulders back into the room and lower my feet on to the ledge. Considering I was slim and fit, and the

103

window was horizontal and narrow, this was not too difficult in itself. The agonizing problem was finding a way to prevent the chair from crashing off the lavatory pan on to the floor. As I swung my knee up the first time the chair slipped and I had to hook it smartly with one foot and ease it back into position.

It remained stationary for my next attempt but when I took my second leg off, it slipped again and remained leaning slightly to one side. It was too late to go back and do anything about it. Hoping fervently that the chair would not fall over until I was well on my way, I wriggled and squirmed until my legs could be lowered slowly on to the ledge outside. Now came the real test. There were only two ways of going along the ledge: face outwards or face to the wall. I concluded that even the smallest of bottoms would push a person with his back to the wall out far enough to over-balance him and so, with arms outstretched in the shape of a cross and with chin pointed in the direction I was heading, I inched my way along, with shirt buttons scraping the brickwork.

One step ... two steps ... there were about fifteen in all. Something cold and metallic came in contact with my left hand. A drainpipe ran down the angle of the wall. I slid my hand round it and edged further to the left. Another stride and I would have to step across the corner. I put an exploratory foot across the void. It touched the sill at right angles to the one on which I had made my way, but only for a moment. Due either to the strain of my Houdini act through the window or, what is more likely, sheer terror, it refused to anchor itself and tapped uncontrollably in a muscular spasm. I pulled it back and felt the whole leg tremble beneath me. After a moment or two I tried again. This time my toes appeared to remain firm but my heel shuddered violently. I pulled it back once more, realizing that it was only a matter of minutes before my knees gave way.

'Get a grip on yourself, Goldsmith,' I wailed to myself mentally.

With a final effort I forced my foot on to the opposite sill and willed it to remain there. I then hauled my right foot along the wall to the drainpipe, to which I held fast with my right hand. After a few moments I felt steady enough to start edging along towards the open window. Before I could reach it, however, I had to pass two other windows, both closed. The first gave me no concern, but as I was poised outside the second a hideous noise paralysed me with fear. 'Grunt – Snarl – Splutter.' A wave of relief swept over me. Some German swine was snoring. I prayed that the occupant of the next room would also be sound asleep.

I paused outside the open window and cautiously peered into the room. To my relief there was no one in it. The light I had seen earlier came from a little stove on which a pot of coffee was bubbling.

Carefully I lowered myself into a little kitchen where officers going on duty in the early hours of the morning could help themselves to coffee. Quickly I looked to see if I could find a knife but there was nothing to be found. With the prospect of escape, my whole being was keyed up and my brain seemed to be working at a tremendous speed. Peering out cautiously, I slipped into the deserted corridor. At the end of it, just before crossing the landing to the stairs, I paused and glanced around the corner. I stepped back with a start. A German soldier was sitting nursing his rifle on a chair propped against the wall. After a moment I realized that he was guarding my room. Fortunately, he had positioned himself near the door looking the other way. Had he been facing me I would have rushed him and tried to throttle him. As it was I decided to cross quietly to the stairs and walk straight down. The soldier had never seen my face and there was no obvious reason for him to think anything was wrong. I stepped smartly across the landing and walked down the stairs as normally as I could – without appearing to hurry and without looking round. The soldier didn't make a sound.

Once I was out of his view I trotted as quickly as possible down to the foyer where, once again, I took stock of the situation. It was deserted. The armchairs were empty and even the N.C.O. clerk had gone from the reception desk. I was just about to cross to the entrance when I heard a cough and a noise. The N.C.O. came out with a pen in his hand, lifted a large book from a table, and returned to a side office. I could see him through the half-open door working on his ledgers. This time I bent double and dashed for the door. I had one more hurdle to surmount, the two sentries. According to regulations, there should have been one on each side of the entrance, and the only movement they were supposed to make was to turn towards each other and either meet or cross as they marched. But at 5 a.m. the regulations were not being enforced. In fact, the soldiers were walking together up and down the long arcade where the Hotel Continentale overhangs the pavement. I could hear the hollow clumping of their boots growing louder as they tramped towards me. I watched them pass and then listened to their footsteps fade as they turned and walked the other way. As it was impossible for me to remain where I was without discovery I walked quickly out of the hotel and stood behind the third pillar with my back in the shadows. The boots now started to clump back again in my direction. When they got near, I slid round the pillar until I was standing with my back to the street. The Germans passed on the other side, deep in conversation. Once they were a reasonable distance away I ran further down the street and took up my position behind another pillar hugging the side farthest away from the guards.

Just over a year later, General de Gaulle was filmed walking down the Rue de Rivoli, past these very pillars, during his triumphal march after the liberation of Paris. But as I slunk in and out of the shadows on that June morning my thoughts were fixed on survival, not victory. When I reached the corner I turned into another street and started to run as fast as I could. Racing over the deserted pavement, I did not stop until I reached the Place de la Concorde where a solitary *sergent de ville* stood looking at the empty square.

Having made sure there were no German patrols lurking around I walked straight up to him without any hesitation.

'Are you a good Frenchman?' I asked him as he stared at my laceless shoes. 'Then give me five francs and don't ask any questions.'

The man did not say a word. He merely reached into his pocket, put a fistful of coins into my hand and turned his back. Two minutes later I was standing with some early-risers waiting for the Metro. When the train arrived I hesitated until the last minute before stepping out of a shadowy corner and once on board I tucked my feet under a seat to hide my tell-tale shoes. I sat hunched up, looking down, but no one took the slightest notice of me. I felt even more conspicuous when I arrived at my destination and headed up the Avenue Victor Hugo, in one of Paris's smartest districts. By now it was broad daylight but still there were not many people on the streets. A quick glance up and down and I turned into the doorway of a select block of flats.

I pressed the door-bell of the basement flat and waited anxiously for the door to be opened. A minute dragged by; then a curious figure appeared, hopping with the aid of a stick, an empty pyjama leg flapping from under his dressing-gown. 'Come inside quickly,' he whispered, but there was no need to tell me. I had pushed past into his tiny bachelor flat before he had finished the sentence.

To an agent on the run, a 'safe' house is a bit like a fox's earth, a haven to be made for when the hounds are close on your heels. The rules regarding these sanctuaries were necessarily stringent, both to maintain their security and to protect the lives of the people who lived in them. Of all the Resistance workers in Europe they had the least glamour and excitement and ran the greatest risks. They had to be totally above suspicion and frequently risked accusations of being collaborators rather than spoil their reputation for being innocent of resistance activities. When the war was over some of these devoted people had to endure insulting inquiries into their loyalty by men whose patriotism blossomed only when the Allies were well and truly established in France. There were plenty of these Twelfth Hour Heroes. Edouard Grosval was not one of them.

9

GROSVAL had little reason to love the Germans and, as later events proved, his cold contempt for them did not go unnoticed. Still, they could hardly expect anything else from a man whose leg had been shattered by an enemy shell in 1940.

According to the strict rules laid down by S.O.E. I should have phoned his flat before my arrival to make sure that the coast was clear. Code phrases had been pre-arranged so that if the Gestapo had raided the flat or if Grosval had had some unreliable visitor, he could have warned me. It was a standard procedure but on this occasion I felt that circumstances allowed me to dispense with it.

As it turned out the coast was clear, although it was soon revealed that I was far from out of danger.

An intense young man, whose pale, lined face betrayed the constant pain he suffered from his wound, Grosval first inspected me for injuries and then, when I had assured him that, apart from a sore and swollen ear, I was unscathed, he busied himself with the coffee pot and produced a bottle with two fingers of cognac in it. I drank the coffee before I attempted a small glass of brandy. I had no idea how my stomach would react to alcohol after the nervous strain of the previous twenty-four hours and was pleased when a warm glow spread through my body.

While I breakfasted on bread and garlic sausage, I filled in the details of my adventure. Grosval listened attentively, sometimes putting in an odd question, sometimes interpolating an ejaculation of surprise. When I reached the champagne incident he shook his head and declared that he would never understand the Germans if he lived to be a hundred years old.

Hopping into the bedroom, Grosval then started to dress, pulling on his trousers which stood against the end of his bed.

'I always leave my false leg inside them,' he explained. 'It's such a chore if you have to fit it into your pants in the morning and it's just as difficult undressing at night. After the war I think I'll have a false leg made for every pair of trousers I've got and stand them in a row in my wardrobe.'

I marvelled at the courage of the man. There could be no ledge climbing or hide-and-seek in the Rue de Rivoli for him if he were caught. And yet he was sticking his neck out further than anyone might reasonably expect him to.

Grosval told me frankly that the police were taking a lot more interest in him than they had done in the past and, although he was fairly certain that they had nothing on him at the moment, it was not a healthy situation. They regarded him as the sort of man who would be a natural enemy and, of course, they were right. It was necessary for me to take very great care.

I got the message.

Boredom, that old enemy, thrived in 'safe' houses. Although it was drilled into every member of S.O.E. that once they were inside a 'safe' house they were not to go out under any circumstances, people broke the rules, driven almost mad by endless hours of inactivity. For a wanted man to take such chances was both foolish and exceedingly selfish. For not only did he put his own life in jeopardy, he also risked being followed to his hideout, perhaps exposing a whole family to trial and deportation. There had been a number of such examples recently, but I made it quite clear that he need have no fears on my account.

'Good,' he said. 'Now we have to work, and work fast.'

Our first job was to make sure that everyone was warned who might possibly be affected by the circumstances leading to my capture. My suspicions about the courier had to be passed on to the Resistance, and to Delphin in particular: London also had to be informed as soon as possible. It was vital that no one else should be in contact with the possible traitor. If I were the first person he had denounced, the Gestapo might well have decided to see what they could get out of me before striking elsewhere and this, in fact, turned out to have been the case. I was not to know this at the time, however, and my sole thought was to send out as many S.O.S. signals as possible, particularly to Lyons, whence Pierre had been intended to take a message after our rendezvous at the café. Grosval needed no urging. Having taken in my instructions he set off to sound the alarm.

I sat alone in the flat listening to the clump and tap of his false leg and walking-stick receding down the Avenue Victor Hugo. According to the tiny alarm clock beside his bed it was now ten o'clock. My hosts of the previous evening would be turning the key of my room in the Hotel Continentale at just that moment. I could imagine the sinking feeling in the stomach of the leader of the strong-arm squad when he realized I was gone. I thought of the blazing anger of Müller, his ingenious display of the previous night now reduced to buffoonery in the eyes of his men. The sentry, too, would no doubt have some explaining to do.

After the boasting in the foyer the previous evening it would soon be all over the German garrison that a spy had escaped. An inquiry was bound to be held. The thought of the hornets' nest that I had stirred up gave me a feeling of intense pleasure as I lay on Grosval's bed, dozing, but unable or afraid to sleep properly. I took comfort in the thought that perhaps Müller and all his minions might end up on the Russian front.

This pleasant dream did not occupy my mind for long. It was dismissed by the more serious contemplation of every possible thing that might have led to my capture and every person who might be affected by it. Time and time again I went through my movements and my contacts and I thanked the Lord that I had not had a regular radio operator. If two of us had been betrayed, many more people would have been involved.

I was brought out of my reverie by the sound of Grosval's stick outside the window. Hastily I rolled off the bed and lay on the floor in case he had anyone with him, but my friend was alone. However, ten minutes later the doorbell rang and a tall, dark young man was admitted. I was introduced to Guillaume Lecointre, son of a famous family of French merchant bankers. In normal times Guillaume would have gone everywhere in Paris by limousine. On this occasion he was wearing bicycle clips.

Guillaume, who was about my own age, was as quick-witted as Grosval was determined. He had already issued some warning based on what Grosval had told him but he wanted to make quite sure that everything necessary was done.

Guillaume also insisted that it was impossible for me to remain in the flat for any length of time; he was aware that in spite of Grosval's disability, he had become too active to avoid suspicion much longer. He would make other arrangements for my concealment and would return within the next two days. I looked at Grosval when Guillaume had finished speaking. He nodded impassively.

'Guillaume is right,' he said. 'It is better if you go.'

My life was already in the hands of these men. There was nothing else to do but obey them.

The next forty-eight hours were among the most uncomfortable I have spent in my life. During the day I waited anxiously for Grosval to return from his normal excursions. If he was a few minutes late I began to dwell upon the possibility of his having been picked up. I listened to the engine of every passing car, wondering whether it sounded like a big black Citroën. While Grosval was in the flat I tried to get some sleep – which at night was impossible. He had fixed up a makeshift bed on the floor beside his own, but if I slept on one side it affected my tender ear, if I slept on the other my good ear, being so close to the ground, picked up every sound from the street.

On top of everything else I was haunted by The Leg. It seemed to have a personality all of its own and I would not have been in the least surprised if it had walked about under its own steam. The last thing I saw at night when I went to bed were Grosval's trousers, one leg standing straight and well creased, ending in a neat, well-polished shoe, while the other hung dejectedly by its side. When I woke in the morning it was the first thing that greeted my eyes. The Leg held an irresistible, morbid fascination for me. Whichever way I turned I always ended up staring at it. Only when Grosval put it on – and I must confess I found the sight equally compelling – did it cease to worry me. Then it was part of him. When it was in sole possession of his trousers it was like sharing the flat with a third person. I felt that The Leg resented my intrusion. It wanted me out.

On the third day The Leg got its way. Guillaume appeared that morning and announced that he had fixed up somewhere else for me to hide. It was on the left bank but there was nothing to worry about. He had obtained transport. *Voila!* He beckoned me into the hall and pointed to the ugliest bicycle I have ever seen. It had obviously made its escape from some police station where it would have borne the fattest of gendarmes without complaint. I remembered with affection the splendid all-aluminium bicycle with drop handle-bars which had carried me during my first assignment as an agent in the south of France.

'Well?' said Guillaume proudly as if he had brought the family Rolls to the door.

'*Formidable!*' was the only reply I could think of.

He beamed.

'There is only one snag,' I continued. 'How do you propose that I am going to get through the streets unscathed. I have no papers of any sort. If we run into a control stop I've had it.'

Control stops were likely to happen in any street at any time of the day. The Germans, with the French police, merely set up a point and everyone passing through had to show his identity card and other permits. Generally speaking there was no bother if you had papers, but they were very effective for picking up shot-down Allied airmen and escaped P.O.W.s.

'Ah, I've thought of that,' said Guillaume cheerfully. 'I shall ride thirty yards in front of you. If there is a *rafle* you will see me halt and can turn off or turn round. It's simple, isn't it?'

Reluctantly I agreed. So Guillaume set off and a few seconds later I followed, having said goodbye to Grosval. It was impossible for him to wave us off but I felt that he was watching from behind the curtains as we rode away. The Leg was once more undisputed master of the field.

If you are six-foot one-inch tall and riding a bicycle made for someone even taller you feel very conspicuous. When at the same time you are wearing exactly the same suit in which your worst enemies last saw you you begin to wonder at your sanity.

It came as something of a surprise to me to discover as we pedalled along that the world had not changed one little bit in the past two days. Everything was going on just as usual, women were shopping, men were sluicing down the parched gutters and the cafés were open. As it was a *jour avec* they were slightly busier. There were only a few indications that the city was in the grip of an invader. Self-consciously I steered my giant vehicle past a parked Wehrmacht lorry loaded with troops in full kit but no one took the slightest notice. Once Guillaume stopped, and I immediately got off to look in a shop window, but he had only paused to shake hands with a friend.

Finally we pulled up outside one of the showpieces of Paris, the Tour d'Argent restaurant, famous then as now for the splendour of its cuisine and the size of its bills. Ignoring the doorman and a couple of German officers who were entering, Guillaume led me to a side door and into a little hall. We left our bicycles there, climbed a short flight of stairs and rang the bell of a flat. In those days a number of flats below and behind the restaurant were available for rent, although today I believe they are used by the staff. The occupier of the apartment at which we called was an attractive Rumanian actress – *artiste dramatique* – in her late thirties.

Madame Tantzy was plump, voluble, patriotic and shrewd. If she was going to put herself in danger, she wanted to be sure it was for a worthwhile person. Hardly had we been introduced than she wanted to know whether I had a wife and, if so, whether we had any family. Once she had been assured that this was so, she became much more tractable. Had I been a single man, she explained later, she would have turned me away to fend for myself. According to her way of looking at things, her life was as valuable as that of any wild youngster in the Resistance. If, however, she was protecting the interests of three or four people, such as a whole family, she regarded the possible sacrifice as being mathematically reasonable. She held out a plump, white hand, which had a remarkably strong grip.

'Enchanté, madame.'

'You are welcome,' she replied. 'My house is your house.'

Guillaume did not linger after making the introductions. He had to get rid of my bicycle before it attracted anyone's attention. He arranged to call from time to time, to keep me informed of what was going on and bring me information. Otherwise I was to lie low and not move out of the flat.

I remained there for thirty-two days.

Madame Tantzy proved to be a remarkable woman. Nothing seemed beyond her talents. She was an expert dressmaker, cook and conversationalist. Coming to Paris from Bucharest in the early 'thirties she had completely fallen for its charms and considered it the only place in the world for a civilized person to live. In this view she was supported by her friend and daily visitor, Monsieur Henri, a most considerate man and a successful jeweller. Madame and Henri had developed that civilized type of relationship which comes only with maturity. The Germans were not civilized and so Madame and Henri would not hesitate to help anyone who wanted them kicked out of Paris. Henri also had a personal score to settle. The Germans had shot off one of his testicles when he was serving with the 71st Infantry Regiment in the Champagne in 1915 and although it had not affected his love life it had given him a considerable fright at the time. They could expect no cooperation from him.

Madame's flat was larger than Grosval's and we were able to make better arrangements for my sleeping quarters. I was installed in what Madame insisted was the box-room, although as far as I could see it was merely an outsize cupboard containing an electric light and a narrow camp bed. For the first few days I divided my time between the box-room and Madame's sitting-room.

Sometimes I listened to the B.B.C., sometimes I helped Madame with her chores and sometimes I read her only book – *Autant en emporte le vent*, which is French for *Gone with the Wind*. Occasionally I would vary this monotonous existence by peering from behind the curtains at the Germans arriving to dine at the restaurant. Madame would then say dramatically that I would be the death of them all by exposing myself to possible discovery but as she invariably joined me in the end I feel that her attitude was more theatrical than candid. There was certainly plenty to watch. Indeed one of the most frequent visitors was one of Madame's former stage friends, the beautiful Rumanian actress Elvire Popesco. She appeared often in the company of immaculately uniformed German staff officers who would hand her down from glittering Mercedes staff cars.

'What sadness,' Madame would say, wiping a tear from her eye. 'Forced to eat with those German pigs.'

I told her that for the life of me I could not understand why she was forced to dine with the Germans but Madame would only shake her head.

'Elvire has to live,' she used to say. 'She is a great actress. What else can she do? And besides she has done much good work for French Jews.'

Faced with this argument I could but agree. At least Elvire never arrived with the Tuesday and Thursday Club, as I christened them. Tuesday and Thursday evenings were the weekly dinner dates for the Paris Gestapo top brass. Two or three black Citroëns would disgorge their sinister occupants, all smartly turned out in civilian clothes, and they would spend a pleasant evening with their girl-friends celebrating their latest arrests, little knowing that two floors below them was a wanted man. To my everlasting regret I never saw Müller among the callers, although it was perhaps just as well as I had the impression that he had a nose for smelling out trouble. Tuesdays and Thursdays always had a slightly tense air about them while I hid at the Tour d'Argent.

On other days Madame used to discuss our domestic affairs.

'Ah, Jean,' she would say, 'you do not know what it is to be a woman, a Rumanian woman. Have you ever known any Rumanian women? Really known them?'

I had to confess that I had not had that pleasure.

'We are not like your Frenchwomen,' she would continue. 'They are hard. They are mercenary. They think only of money. The women of Rumania have souls. We have hearts. We are generous.'

From this the conversation generally worked its way round to my own lonely existence and finally to my comfort.

'Ah, Jean, are you sure you are comfortable in that tiny room. I feel so mean each night when I am lying in my beautiful, soft bed.'

The truth was that I was damned uncomfortable in my cupboard and not only because of its dimensions. For I was not the sole occupant. There was Lazslo too.

Lazslo was Madame's large and supercilious Siamese cat. At night he slept at the bottom of Madame's bed, a miniature four-poster with a splendid blue curtain all round it. Like Madame he left the flat rarely. Like The Leg he regarded it as his own kingdom and ignored both Henri and myself. For this I was not unthankful as I have an instinctive dislike of cats and would cheerfully have ignored Lazslo in return. This, however, was impossible. I was constantly reminded of his existence because of the presence in my

115

cupboard of a large sand-covered tray which he used as a lavatory. During the day the box-room door was left ajar so that he could get in and out when nature called. To catch sight of him disappearing purposefully inside after a good meal was a distressing experience. The baleful stare he gave me on his return did nothing to alleviate matters. From time to time I was tempted to empty the tray myself, but I refrained from doing so for the simple reason that I would have had to show myself. I had no desire to give Lazslo the pleasure of having me returned to the mercies of the Gestapo. As good manners prevented me from drawing Madame's attention to the problem I suffered in silence. Besides had I mentioned my ordeal, Madame might have got the impression that I wished to share her bed with her. Certainly we were becoming very knowledgeable about each other's private life. I had to listen to her fears for Henri for a start. He was not as young as he used to be. (He was then 60.) If only I had known him a few years earlier. Then he was full of vigour despite his old wound. Now he made love only now and again.

Personally I thought that this was a grave calumny on Henri. For a gentleman of advancing years his sexual prowess seemed to be more than adequate. He seemed to find the strength and the time most afternoons to prove his affections – as I knew to my cost.

After a pleasant lunch and a bottle of wine – Henri could get anything – he would indicate delicately that he and Madame had things of a personal matter to discuss. A less sensitive person might have disappeared with her into the bedroom and vanished beneath those big blue curtains without a word, but I realized that Henri thought that it was improper for me to be in the sitting-room while he was making love. So I would make an excuse and say that I had some reading to catch up on and disappear into my dungeon where I would shut love out and lock the fragrance of Lazslo in. The length of time I spent in there can be gauged from the fact that I read *Gone with the Wind* five times before I left.

Had I stayed in the flat much longer I think that I would have been forced to seek refuge in Madame's bed, as even her own pungent perfumes, which filled the place day and night with the atmosphere of an eastern market, were preferable to the stench of that cat. As it was, I was driven on occasions to take unnecessary risks rather than remain in Lazslo's vicinity. Once when almost overpowered by the aroma of my box-room I insisted on taking a walk along the bank of the Seine in order to get some fresh air. Our little promenade came to a sudden end when almost automatically I spat as we passed the Hotel de Ville. Madame was horrified.

'Why did you do that, Jean?' she demanded in a tense whisper, clutching my arm in her fright.

'Because they are all bastards,' was my reply as Madame dragged me unwillingly homewards.

It was a small incident but it made me realize that the long period of confinement was getting on my nerves. Occasionally Guillaume Lecointre called discreetly to inquire after my health and bring me news but what I wanted was the opportunity and the means to get on the move again.

Even the attentions of one of Guillaume's couriers, a pretty girl called Nicole, could not eradicate the boredom of being cooped up, especially as the chances of being recaptured seemed to recede as the days went by. Pierre, the man who betrayed me, and my principal source of danger had been assassinated by one of the Resistance's teams of trained killers – *équipes de tueurs* – within three days of my arrest. I did not think that he would last once it had been ascertained beyond all doubt that he had sold me to the Gestapo. The killer teams normally did no other form of Resistance work, and were therefore above suspicion. Their numbers included harmless-looking under-developed students and one or two anaemic girls. I got the impression that the weaker they looked the more deadly they were.

Ironically another thing in my favour was the sad fact that the Germans were having a field day against the Prosper circuit and were roping in agents and Resistance workers all over Paris. This meant that the Gestapo had their hands full and would not be paying any special attention to my own whereabouts.

Clothes had been provided to replace those in which I had escaped – I could now pass for a businessman – and once I had false papers I could chance my arm (or my neck) in the world again.

On the fourth week of my incarceration I got the opportunity I had been waiting for. Madame was told by Guillaume to go to a certain shop in Les Halles, the Paris market which was then in the centre of the city, and buy some fish. She was also told not to forget to ask for any cigarettes that were going.

When she returned she said that the man had been kind enough to let her have a packet of ten. While she cooked the fish I examined the cigarettes and then slit one carefully down the side. My heart jumped for joy when I read the message written on the cigarette paper. My departure was being arranged. Papers were on their way.

The following day that brave old man Monsieur Henri pulled up outside the flat in a tiny two-seater contraption powered by a motor-cycle engine and, after I had endured a tearful farewell performance by Madame, chug-chugged off to the Gare d'Austerlitz, where he dropped me and wished me luck.

Free from the persecution of Lazslo and Madame Tantzy's scent, I felt exhilarated, but the sight of my reflection in a window had a calming effect on me. As a parting gift Henri had given me an imposing black trilby hat, which carried with it an air of solemnity that transcended any emotion the wearer might feel. I reduced my pace to speed commensurate with unaccustomed and new-found dignity. Normally I did not wear a hat – uniform excepted – and I felt very conspicuous and a thorough phoney. I hoped that my physical appearance would be changed by the hat as much as my personality. There could be no doubt that the Gestapo had circulated my picture, taken from my false papers when I was arrested, to every one of its men in the city and that my countenance would also have featured largely in the French equivalent of the *Police Gazette*. Every minute I remained in my home town reduced my chances of survival.

The greatest test would be the passage of the ticket barrier at the station, where the Germans kept a permanent watch for wanted men. There was a queue at the booking office and I shuffled slowly towards the window praying fervently that the God of Black Hats would accept me as one of his own adherents just for this one day. After that I would never commit the sacrilege of appearing in public again in such distinguished headgear. The deity appeared to have heard me because when a whole file of German soldiers in uniform tramped through the station foyer and pushed through the queue just where I was standing the leader of them actually muttered a polite 'Excuse me, monsieur,' although I was already stepping smartly to one side.

Once I had obtained my ticket I plunged into the middle of the throng pressing through to the platform.

Two stony-faced individuals in light-weight suits and straw hats were standing by the ticket inspector and surveying the crowd. They had Gestapo stamped all over them and I swallowed hard. Suddenly one of them stepped forward and tapped the shoulder of a young woman in front of me. She looked round in alarm, but he merely pointed to the ground behind her and she picked up a magazine she had dropped. I took this opportunity to squeeze past. No one said a word and I thrust my small suitcase in front of me and barged my way on to the train and into the crowded corridor.

Standing there as we rattled through the suburb I felt a sense of achievement and a considerable amount of relief. Paris had become a forbidden city as far as I was concerned. There would be no second opportunity for escape if I was caught again. The Gestapo would not thank me for making fools of their brethren and no doubt they had mentally reserved something special in the way of treatment for me if I fell into their hands once more. I hoped that Red Hair and his pals had by now arrived at the Russian front.

A voice interrupted my thoughts. A smartly-dressed man of middle age on my left asked me if I could possibly move up to make more room. I squeezed along as requested and gradually was drawn into conversation. We talked about the weather, the war situation and rationing (which did not seem to have done him any harm) and finally about the black market. I was just about to air some of my views on the subject when my eye fell on the man's left hand, which was resting on the window rail. Pointing to a large gold signet ring on one of his podgy fingers I asked politely: 'Excuse me but isn't that the *croix gammée*?'

The croix gammée, or crooked cross, was what the French called the swastika but my fellow traveller was not offended.

'That's right,' he said.

'Are you a German then?' I continued. 'For your French is perfect.'

'It should be,' he replied. 'I have lived here for fifteen years.'

He explained that he came from a South German town and had set up business in France before the war. Now he was working for 'a government department'. I did not need three guesses to find out which one.

After ten minutes or so, I made an excuse about looking for a friend at the other end of the train and pushed my way down there. The man with the gold swastika did not pursue me but I remained on edge throughout the rest of the journey. I had no doubt at all that he was a Gestapo man, and a clever one at that. Had I given the game away I wondered? Should I have stayed with him and tried to brazen it out? These thoughts plagued me until I reached my destination, a small country station about ten miles from Vichy.

I had been told that I would be contacted there by a man wearing plus fours, but apart from an elderly porter there was no one in sight. I handed over my ticket and walked to the entrance where I paused at the door. It looked as though I might have to wait and I did not like the idea. Waiting attracted attention. The porter came out and stared at me curiously. Then, in the distance, I heard a powerful car engine. My apprehension grew as a big black car swept into view and drew up opposite. For a second I thought that the man I had encountered on the train had set a trap for me. Then a solitary figure got out of the car and came towards me with his hand outstretched. He was wearing plus fours. 'Awfully sorry I'm late, old chap,' he said as he took my suitcase. 'Difficult confinement. All right now though. Come along.'

Le Toubib, as my doctor friend was known throughout the area, sheltered me for the next two months. According to my cover story he was an old friend to whom I had been sent to convalesce after a serious illness. Country air was what the specialist in Paris was supposed to have ordered . . . and had he existed I would have agreed whole-heartedly.

Paris was getting tougher every minute and there seemed to be no end to the wave of arrests. Three days after I left the shop-keeper who passed on the cigarette message to Madame Tantzy at Les Halles was arrested and soon afterwards shot. Nicole was pulled in for questioning but was released after a couple of un-pleasant days in custody. Only Madame and the old gentleman carried on undisturbed two floors beneath the fat bottoms of the

Germans indulging themselves in the Tour d'Argent. The country-side seemed a restful place indeed after the deadly pressures of the city.

Le Toubib was a key figure among Resistance workers in the area. Because he could get around in his car without suspicion he made an excellent messenger. He was also available to transport people if necessary. Primarily, however, he provided a head-quarters for Colonel Henri Zeller, then head of the Giraudist Secret Army. (Zeller continued his clandestine activities long after the war and was jailed for his part in the Algerian conspiracy. I was pleased to see he has since been released.)

Zeller arrived at Le Toubib's house shortly after I did. With a red face and bristling moustache he looked more like the popular idea of a British Blimp than a Frenchman, but closer acquaintance was to reveal a highly intelligent mind. For Zeller my arrival was opportune as it provided him with a staff to deal with problems in his frequent absences and someone to help him with the coding and decoding of numerous messages.

Of all the Frenchmen I met, Zeller was the most security conscious. Meticulously he burnt every scrap of the one-time code pads after use. He never used the same railway station twice running and he carefully staggered his time of arrival at Le Toubib's house. Often I took over from Le Toubib as Zeller's chauffeur, running him from one point to another. Together we searched for potential dropping zones and landing grounds for Lysanders. When Zeller was away I spent my time giving sabotage lessons to small selected teams. If there was any problem at this time it was being discreet inside the doctor's home rather than outside, as he was having an affair with his wife's sister who lived with the family. The fact that both the women were Chinese made the situation all the more bizarre. But following the pattern set by the rest of the household I gave no indication that domestic arrangements were anything other than normal.

Ironically, Le Toubib survived his domestic complications and the war, only to die after the Liberation of the complaint which had been ascribed to me. I did not see him again after I left his home, on instructions from London, in September 1943.

My destination was, almost unbelievably, Paris. Considering the success of current Gestapo purges and the shattering of the

Prosper circuit, this appeared to me to be an unnecesary risk but I had no option, so off I went. My reluctance was increased by an arrangement to meet Guillaume Lecointre in a smart restaurant for dinner. I had no wish to find Herr Müller at the next table. Fortunately he appeared to be dining elsewhere that night (either that or having someone tortured) and all went well. Instead I had the pleasure of meeting Monsieur Robert Mathé-Dumaine, owner of Kargal, winner of the Grand Steeplechase de Paris that year. In his company I could feel as safe as anywhere in France. Monsieur Mathé-Dumaine maintained a perfectly correct relationship with all factions, at least on the surface. His house was therefore a haven for agents or men on the run. For three days I enjoyed his hospitality at his home in the Rue Marceau and caught up on the latest racing news. Kargal, he promised me, would come to England and be trained by me after the war. I was impressed by Robert's faith in final victory but even more by his certainty that I would personally live to see it. I wished I could have been as confident when I took my leave of him and set off for Angers with orders to await a Lysander to take me home to England. Guillaume Lecointre was to travel with me.

The pick-up was once again arranged by the ubiquitous Déricourt. Somewhere around midnight on 17 September I found myself standing with a small group of figures with suitcases in the shadow of a hedge in the heart of the country. Other dark figures flitted across the make-shift landing ground. As a distant droning grew louder, all movement ceased and faces turned expectantly skywards. Then with a whirring snarl, a great black bat appeared over a distant wood and swept in a low circle around the site, casting an enormous shadow over the moonlit meadow. As the circuit was repeated Déricourt flashed a red torch at the plane . . . the letter 'E' in morse code. A light winked back in reply. Promptly the Lysander banked, then swooped steeply and raced swiftly over the grass towards two more red torches glowing at the upwind end of the field. There it turned and came bumping back towards us, swung round again and stopped ready to take off immediately if necessary. As we made our way towards it, the door opened and a figure stepped into the pink light reflected on the underside of the broad wing directly above one of the ground signal torches. Members of the reception committee hurried to help with the cases being handed out by another agent inside the plane. The luggage was promptly whisked away to be handed over at a safe house the following day, the infiltrating agents made for the transport which had been laid on for them, and Guillaume and I climbed into the cramped interior of the plane. The door was closed and we fastened our seat belts as engine revs increased and we took off smartly into the night. Below, the landing lights went out one by one and the field, which was still the scene of urgent but invisible activity, blended with the rest of the peaceful countryside.

'Was one of those infiltrating agents a woman?' Guillaume asked me later as we droned over the glittering Channel towards England. I was unable to tell him. All my concentration had been devoted to making the landing drill go through properly. Later I was told that among the agents who had been landed at the Angers strip at this time was Yolande Beekman (code name Yvonne) a wireless operator bound for the Musician circuit at St. Quentin. She was arrested by the Gestapo four months later and in September 1944, nearly a year to the day after she landed in France, she was shot with three other British girl agents in the execution yard at Dachau. The same plane which flew me to safety may have been the one which took her to her death. That night, however, the identity of the incoming party was hidden from me. They were merely mysterious figures who scurried off into the night as quickly as we, with equal anonymity took their places.

An attractive F.A.N.Y. met us when we touched down in England, and took us straight to the familiar hotel in Kensington. After a brief rest and a shave I was picked up again and driven to Orchard Court. Once more I was given a hearty welcome by Buckmaster, distinguished by the comment of Selwyn Jepson who said: 'I can't understand Goldsmith, he always comes back looking better than when he went away.' A slightly less friendly attitude was taken by a representative of M.I.5 who wanted to take me off to 'debrief' me at what was quaintly described as The Patriotic School. Buckmaster would not hear of it and said that he regarded me as one of his best agents and that I was going home for a rest. As an afterthought he told me that I had been awarded a *palme* to my Croix de Guerre.

123

The M.I.5. man consented rather reluctantly and I disappeared before anyone could change their mind. London already had a full report of my activities, via Zeller, Lecointre and my own messages, but it was quite natural for the internal security people to be wary of any person who had spent any time at all in the hands of the Gestapo. There was always the possibility that an agent could have been 'turned' – persuaded to work for the other side – although under the circumstances the Germans were hardly likely to allow such a prize to return home again.

In fact, at the very moment I was setting out on indefinite leave, one of the men who had trained with me was being used as a tool of the Germans. Of all people it was Gilbert Norman (code name Archambaud) who had been so proud of his physical prowess and who had phoned Orchard Court from Ringway the night we got rid of Polydore, our objectionable conducting officer. Although no one in London told me officially I learned from various French contacts that he had been captured by the Gestapo when they broke the Prosper circuit at the end of June 1943. After the war it was revealed that he had co-operated with the Gestapo having being convinced that they knew nearly everything about the F section of S.O.E. *S.O.E. in France* gives credence to the story that Gilbert's nerve went after he sent a wireless message to London following his capture which contained a special danger signal indicating that he was working under German control. In reply London is alleged to have told him that he had left out his correct security check and that he should take more care in the future. Whether this is true or not I am not in a position to say. But it is not impossible for even a highly-trained agent to allow himself to be mentally broken by men cleverer than himself, and many of the Gestapo officers were remarkably cunning. The capture of Gilbert Norman and Francis Suttill, who ran the circuit, led to literally scores of men and women being arrested.

Norman, who had been Suttill's wireless operator, later turned up in the Avenue Foch offices of the Gestapo where his presence was used to demoralize captured agents after their arrest. There was no need under the circumstances for Norman to have pointed a finger at the suspect. The mere sight of him sitting behind a desk in comfort, perhaps drinking a cup of coffee, would have been enough to convince most men that all had been betrayed. I have sometimes wondered how I would have reacted if I had been confronted with this situation. I have little doubt that it would have been a shattering experience.

How Norman was induced to play such a role has never been fully explained. It availed him little in the end for when his usefulness was exhausted he was thrown into Fresnes prison and a year later executed in a German concentration camp. Although he was much respected and had many friends in S.O.E., I personally formed the opinion before we completed our training that he should never have been sent into the field. For a start, I thought he looked Jewish and therefore was likely to attract attention. But my main worry was that he was too sure of himself. An agent who wishes to survive should take nothing on trust, not even himself. However, in September 1943, I knew none of the unhappy details of Gilbert Norman's actions, only that he had been arrested. I recalled at the time that he had told me with a certain amount of pride during training that one of his relatives was a conscientious objector and I wondered how he felt about it now.

10

'JEAN de la Lune a rejoint Annette et Gaie,' I repeat. 'Jean de la Lune a rejoint Annette et Gaie.'

The words were intoned undramatically by the announcer broadcasting messages from London to occupied Europe. They meant something to only a very few people. To Madame Tantzy and Henri, who had listened every night since my escape, they revealed that their grave risks had not been in vain. I know that Madame wept when she heard them. To Zeller and Déricourt it meant another successful Lysander operation. To me it meant that I was out of a job.

Few people are more useless in a war than a spy whose face is known to his worst enemies. As my photograph and description had been widely circulated there was no point in my going back to France and so I was sent on indefinite leave. I spent the first fortnight with my wife at her mother's home near Chester. Then we came back to London where we stayed in one of the S.O.E. flats in Kensington, saw what sights there were to be seen and caught up on the news. Very little of it was good; much of it was decidedly bad.

First of all I learned that Amps, the jockey, had been arrested in the big round-up of agents in the Prosper circuit. His luck had been right out. Because he had been so hopeless at dealing with codes and other routine work he had officially been allowed to ease out of the clandestine activities of his comrades and had gone to live a normal life with his wife. But when the Gestapo closed in Amps was implicated through papers found on other agents and was arrested. How such an unsuitable person was sent into the field puzzles me to this day. I refuse to believe that we were that hard up.

Not long afterwards I learned with some bitterness that John Young, for whom I'd had so many fears, had also been taken in a particularly nerve-shattering fashion. His wife had given another agent a letter to deliver to her husband. This agent, or one of his couriers, still had the letter on him when he was caught. The result was the dispatch of a German counter-agent to make contact with John who was working in the Dijon area. Once the double agent had established John's identity by handing over the letter it was only a very short time before the Germans seized not only John but Diana Rowden who was working with him. To take out such an incriminating letter was an act of criminal negligence for which the outgoing agent and his conducting officer must share the blame. No wife who had not been in France herself could have appreciated the danger or she would never have risked such a fatal breach of security. The letter should have been refused point blank by the courier or accepted and destroyed.

Whether John Young would have remained free throughout the war if the letter had never been sent no one can say, but I always felt that the odds were stacked against him. With his obvious foreign accent he needed to be protected constantly, either by hiding him away or simply by not working at his job as a wireless operator. And John was far too proud to accept the latter course.

Towards the end of October, I was summoned to Orchard Court and sounded out about another mission. Would I like to go to Algiers to work for the staff of the North African section of S.O.E. (code-named Massingham)? After my previous glimpse of conditions out there, the outsize headquarters of numerous Allied forces and the red tape, I was not exactly over the moon about the project, but as there was little alternative I agreed. This delighted my wife who would at least know that I was working in uniform and in a position to keep her informed about my well-being instead of her having to rely upon the cryptic notifications sent out by S.O.E. to the relatives of agents in the field. These so-called 'good news letters' merely said that the authorities were continuing to receive good reports if the agent was in good health, became vague if an agent vanished; and if the worst happened, they usually stopped altogether – if it was considered a threat to security to reveal that an agent had been killed. As it was not intended that I should operate in the field from North Africa there seemed little prospect of Tiny receiving any more dramatic communications on my account. It was just as well that she was spared the nagging worry she had endured on my two previous tours of duty because it was about this time we heard that Gilbert Norman had fallen into German hands. The Germans had also succeeded in putting their finger on Staggs and although they never proved his association with S.O.E., they neutralized him so that he made no further contribution to subversive activities.

The facts in themselves present a serious challenge to the quality of S.O.E.'s methods of selection and training. Of the five agents who completed the course with me at Ringway in 1942 I alone remained at the disposal of the organization. Within a year all five of us had either been betrayed to, or traced by, the German counter-intelligence services. Three of our number were either inside or destined for concentration camps; one of us, Staggs, was effectively out of the war until his area of France was liberated, and my effectiveness had been compromised because my identity was known. Had the Germans been just a little more thorough they might have wiped us out completely. As it was they had struck a severe blow because Staggs, Young and Norman were all wireless operators – they had gone for further training after I was sent to the Riviera – and as such were an incalculable loss to our side.

Worse news followed the bad tidings I'd already heard. The irrepressible Sidney Jones had also been taken. Although warned that the Gestapo were watching his French wife's home in Paris, he had risked a visit to her. The Germans sprang their trap and Sidney disappeared from view for ever.

It was with this disturbing news fresh in my mind that I took the plane to Algiers three weeks before Christmas, 1943. Fortunately I was soon to have plenty of other problems to take my mind off the fate of my former comrades.

On the face of it, the S.O.E. organization in North Africa was a muddled affair, without the refinements of its European counterpart. But it was new by comparison and had been called upon to perform equal, and even heavier, tasks. North Africa, with its well developed airfields, was ideally placed to feed arms and ammunition to the Resistance forces in the south of France, now being prepared for the invasions to come. With demands increasing every day there was more than enough to do.

I found the headquarters of Massingham at the Club des Pins at Guyotville just west of Algiers. Carrying on the traditions of S.O.E. in Britain the powers-that-be had taken over a collection of exclusive country villas where the rich used to enjoy themselves before the war. Unfortunately it soon became apparent that little of the luxury of by-gone days had lingered on. Instead of sharing a room with, say, one other man, as at Beaulieu, I found myself uncomfortably accommodated with four other officers. That in itself was no great hardship, but as I settled down to give a series of lectures to the agents quartered at Guyotville, other and more important snags became apparent. Although the British staff had their own mess and reasonable conditions, the newly-trained French agents were treated more like private soldiers. They had no batmen and they had to queue for their meals at a cookhouse. As most of them had been officers in the French regular army they did not take kindly to being treated like this and responded indifferently to discipline.

They were also heartily sick of the attitude of some of the British intelligence officers, who seemed just able to read a map but could do precious little else, especially when it came to diplomatic relations with the French.

The total lack of recreational facilities did little to improve the situation. It was not too bad while agents were on courses, when they got all the exercise they needed. The trouble started when they had completed their training and were standing by to be dropped into France. In London, no such problem existed. The splendid system of billeting waiting agents in flats in the capital saw to that. But Guyotville was no metropolis and a man could not be expected to hang about there indefinitely. It frequently happened that if an operation was laid on at short notice an agent or two would be missing. Immediately I would have to drive into Algiers and start searching the bars, brothels and restaurants. After I had dragged an agent out of a girl's bed for the third time in a week I suggested to Commander Francis Brooks-Richards, the head of the section, that we ought to think of something else to amuse the French while they were waiting for action.

Soon afterwards, with his agreement and approval, I set up a holding school at Sidi Ferruch. It consisted of a six neat little *cabanons* – bungalows set on stilts in the sea. Henceforth an agent who had completed the rest of his training would come to me for parachute jumps, cover stories and documentation. Apart from swimming, there was basketball and other sports, decent eating facilities and servants. With only two men to a bungalow I could cope with a dozen agents at a time quite comfortably. By a further stroke of luck I bumped into a young French officer in Algiers who revealed that his family lived at La Trappe, about three miles from Sidi Ferruch. On being invited to lunch with Monsieur and Madame Borgeaud I learned that my hosts were the biggest wine growers in Algiers – and I scored a big hit by taking with me as a present a couple of white loaves baked by my Spanish cook.

On the production of such rarities I instantly became the most popular man in Algeria and henceforth the cabanons at Sidi Ferruch flowed with the finest vintages. The agents at the holding school were made most welcome at the Borgeaud home and riding some of the firm's 150 horses became a regular pastime. With the introduction of dances, attended by members of the women's services, all straying by agents 'on the brink' ceased. It was just as well, for intense pressures were building up, both political and military.

The position of the French in North Africa has never been an easy one for the British to understand. Little wonder, considering that the French couldn't explain it themselves. To make any sense of it one has to go back to the Armistice of 1940, which many Frenchmen regarded as a legitimate settlement with Hitler, however tragic and undesirable they may have thought it. It was, after all, the third time in seventy years that they had signed a peace treaty with Germany. In keeping their North African possessions the French were able to preserve some independence of spirit, and a considerable part of the French Army regarded as binding the oath it subsequently swore to Marshal Pétain. Until the Allied invasion at the end of 1942, therefore, the differences between the French factions themselves were fairly straightforward. There were those who regarded Pétain as the betrayer of France and there were those who regarded the *status quo* as something to be endured.

In the two years that passed between the Armistice and the

Allied invasion of North Africa the conformists had plenty of opportunity to consolidate their position. The actions of the Royal Navy in attacking the remnants of the French fleet at Dakar, Mers-el-Kebir and in Syria and Madagascar did nothing to endear the British to their former allies. A state of distrust bordering on hatred existed, the depth of which can be judged from the fact that the commander of the powerful French squadron holed up in Alexandria since 1940 refused to join the Allied cause even after North Africa had fallen to the Anglo-American forces.

Matters were even more complicated by the accidental presence in Algiers at the time of the invasion of Admiral Jean François Darlan, the commander-in-chief of the Vichy armed forces, on a visit to his son who was ill in hospital. Darlan, who made no secret of his contempt for the British, was probably the most powerful man in France at that time; such was his influence that the greater part of his troops in Algeria would have obeyed orders to go on fighting against the British regardless of the careful emphasis placed on co-operation with the Americans. Influenced, however, by the German attempt to seize the French fleet at Toulon and by the invasion of the *Zone Libre*, Darlan agreed with General Eisenhower that he should take the civilian post of High Commissioner for Algeria, thus successfully freezing out General Giraud whom the Allies had expected to have the job. Instead Giraud was made Commander-in-Chief of the French forces, a somewhat empty appointment for Eisenhower was in effect commander of all troops in the area.

The appointment of Darlan has since been defended by the Americans as fortuitous, because he was on the spot at the time and inevitable because of military priorities. (One is tempted to wonder how much this policy of expediency has influenced them in Vietnam.) Others have regarded it as a callous betrayal of the Free French who had fought on since 1940.

Whatever the truth may be it is fairly clear that no one considered what effect such a liaison would have on the work already done to organize the Resistance forces inside France. The Giraudists, mainly regular army officers ashamed of the Armistice, felt betrayed. Many of them had risked their lives to create a secret army ready to play its part in the liberation of their country. Not a few had died. Now they saw their revered leader thrown over to make way for a man who, in their eyes, was a tool of the despised Hitler-lover, Pierre Laval, the Vichy premier.

So the Giraudists felt betrayed, particularly by the Americans. In that they were not alone. For the communists, who formed a significant section of the Resistance inside France, regarded Darlan as one of the arch-enemies of the Soviet Union. That anyone who had co-operated with the Germans should be so lightly accepted into the Allied camp was anathema to them. The whole thing smelled of treachery and they asked themselves who could be trusted. Certainly it would have to be a very clever American to sell them anything after this.

The third big Resistance movement to be disenchanted by the affair were the Gaullists. They wanted nothing to do with Giraud, but at least they respected him. No one could deny that he was a patriot. But Darlan! This was an unforgivable insult. It is doubtful whether General de Gaulle ever forgot it and it may well have influenced his later dealings with the Americans.

The assassination of Darlan on Christmas Eve 1942 and the summary execution by firing squad of his young murderer could not undo the damage inflicted. It was now too late for General Giraud to be effective. He had been shown to be a man without power and was treated as such.

Political dissension and lack of central direction played havoc with the Resistance forces during the following months. Each organization was at loggerheads with the next. No man could rely on his neighbour. Ordinary French citizens were baffled. Those who had believed that Giraud had large Resistance forces at his command could not understand why he had been received so coolly in Algiers. People who had listened sympathetically to Darlan's doctrine of co-existence with the Germans were still bewildered by his death.

Once the sands had settled after the storm, the tide was set for General de Gaulle although his supporters were still far from convinced that the Allies meant to play fair by him.

Although I was well aware of all these tensions I was not prepared for a schism as deep as was revealed to me during my stay in North Africa. In particular, I was surprised by reports of the conduct of the various maquis groups.

Maquis is a Corsican word for undergrowth in which bandits conceal themselves. In the war it came to mean an armed band of French guerillas. There the general application of the word ceases. Partisan groups could be of any size and have any political ideals. They might have any sort of para-military organization. Their leaders could be colonels or cowhands. Their only common objective was the deliverance of France from the Nazis; but they did not always make that their first priority. A number of reports came in of one maquis betraying another to the Germans in order to achieve their own ends. Scores between Left and Right wings of the French political scene were occasionally paid off in this way. On top of this there were other difficulties to be faced.

The irregular nature of the maquis made discipline a major problem, and one which was never really solved. In industrialized France and the big cities such problems did not arise because the work of the Resistance was fundamentally different. A worker in the Renault factory could pass faulty castings while he was doing his job. A labourer on a bunker could add the wrong proportion of sand to cement.

If a train was derailed the gangers could take their time and lose their equipment. At the end of the day nearly all of the resisters went home and ate their rations. Other workers did normal jobs during the day and perhaps helped a sabotage team at night or went to a weapons class. They were still being paid and eating tolerably, if not well.

The men in the country Resistance had none of these basic essentials. At night they slept out, sometimes under brushwood coverings in the forests, sometimes in crude huts. They drew no pay. They lived on short rations. As long as there were only a few people involved this was no great problem but as the war dragged on, and more and more young Frenchmen fled from the towns to escape forced labour in Germany or on the Todt construction works, the numbers of each maquis grew.

This was just the opposite of the aims of the Allied commanders. Experts in guerilla warfare laid down that each maquis should remain as small as possible until about six weeks before the invasion of the south of France. In the meantime the maquisards should be trained in their homes in the use of weapons ready for the call that would send them into the hills and woods where they would be formed into fighting units.

It was a policy of perfection. The longer the invasion was delayed the bigger the maquis grew. Their clothes wore out. They went hungry. Some got so fed up that they went home where not a few fell into Germans hands and were made to talk. Others raided French villages, commandeering food, wine and clothes. Sometimes they offered a 'bond of recognition' to be reclaimed from the government after the war (no one specified which government); others offered I O Us and promises. A few behaved like gangsters and took what they wanted at the point of a gun. Little wonder that in some areas the French were as afraid of their own maquisards as of the Germans.

I gained the clearest picture of this unhappy situation from a visitor who arrived at the Club des Pins to see Brooks-Richards and his second-in-command, Robert Searle. The situation in the south of France had been deteriorating for some time and F section wanted to get to the bottom of it if they could. Arms, ammunition, instructors and stores were available, along with the planes to carry them, but nobody wanted to see the French using them against each other. In search of a solution, Brooks-Richards had called over one of the leading maquis chiefs in the south, Commandant Pierre-Michel Rayon, who bore the code-name Archiduc but who was known to all his friends as P-M.

I have not seen the name Rayon in any of the accounts I have read of the exploits of the Resistance. But of all the men I met during the war I found him the most impressive.

He was 29 when we first met, six years my junior. About five-feet seven-inches tall, with thick black hair, he was lean and hard and direct, with a strong Marseilles accent. His slit-like blue eyes never left the face of any person he was talking to. It would not be too much to say that he had the appearance of a wolf. Considering that he had been hunting and been hunted by the Germans since long before the war this was hardly surprising.

P-M.'s war with the Nazis began as a student of 19 when he asked his father to let him have a passport so that he could accompany a football team to Italy. Having obtained the passport he promptly set off to see some anti-Fascist friends who were operating in Prague, and there had his first taste of subversive work.

134

Formal soldiering did not appeal to him and when he was called up at the beginning of the war he was so disgusted at the chaos he saw at the depot that he went home for a fortnight 'to let them sort themselves out'. When he came back no one had missed him. I don't think he was really surprised when France collapsed.

P-M. had opened a bar at Antibes which he used as the headquarters for a *reseau* of Polish officers and N.C.O.s who had drifted to the Riviera. Locking the door in the evening, they would hold meetings far into the night. In the end the local police got worried and P-M. received a hint that if he didn't get out soon the Vichy government would be sending someone to arrest him.

He at once set out for the Spanish frontier accompanied by his wife, who was pregnant at the time. P-M. was turned back at the border but she managed to get through and eventually reached Lisbon.

Undeterred he tried again and got through. He then walked two-thirds of the way through Spain pretending to be deaf, dumb and daft, his only document being a railway ticket to Lisbon. Gaping vacantly, he would show this to the police whenever he was stopped, gesturing in the direction in which he was going. With such experience behind him, P-M. was a natural for subversive training when he eventually reached England. This training made a great impression on him, and later he never failed to give full credit for it.

At the time I met him, P-M. had 1,000 men under his command in the hilly wilderness on both sides of the Rhône, north of Avignon. Gard, west of the river, and Vaucluse, east of it, are the districts at the mouth of a broad pass that lies between the Massif Central and the French Alps. It was up and down this route that the Germans defending the south of France would have to pass in the event of an invasion. Massingham's role was to make sure that the maquis in those areas had enough arms and ammunition. The problem, as we have seen, was that many of the maquis leaders were at loggerheads with each other. But Brooks-Richards knew they all had great respect for P-M. and had asked him to North Africa to discuss the possibility of taking back an English officer to arrange supply drops and to organize the distribution of food, arms and money.

I was originally brought in simply as an interpreter. I had to explain that the British had no interest in French internal politics and that our sole concern was to kick the Germans out of France as soon as possible. To this end we would arrange for him and his fellow maquis leaders to be supplied with whatever was necessary. When the war was over, it would be for the French to settle their differences themselves. That, I assured him, was official British policy.

Soon afterwards P-M. announced that he would be happy to take any British officer Brooks-Richards liked to name back to France as long as his name was John Goldsmith. Brooks-Richards, who had got what he wanted, raised no objection. He could always get someone else to run the holding wing but people who could talk French to Pierre-Michel Rayon were hard to find.

The partisan attitude of P-M. became embarrassingly evident a day or so later when he saw my name on Orders on the notice board where it was announced that 'Captain J. Goldsmith, General Service List' was being posted on active service.

He calmly got to work with a pen, promoted me to major and restored me to the strength of the Royal Armoured Corps whose badges I still wore. Fortunately the powers-that-be took it in good part and when I set off they took the hint and made me up to major.

The plan of operation was quite straightforward. I was to be dropped in uniform into the Vaucluse and stay with P-M. One of the wireless operators already working for him would relay requests for arms and ammunition to Guyotville where Brooks-Richards would do the rest. From time to time I would be required to fly back to North Africa to report on my progress and make any suggestions I might have. Some idea of the international nature the war had assumed since the early days can be gauged from the fact that the three other officers who made the trip with me and were going on to other maquis were a Canadian, an American and a Frenchman.

P-M. himself set off two days ahead of us. Before he left he turned to Brooks-Richards and said with a charming smile: 'Don't worry about Jean. He will go everywhere with me. I will look after him personally. I'll even share my bed with him if it is necessary!'

11

A GALE tugged and buffeted my trousers as I sat with my legs dangling through the hatch of the lumbering Stirling bomber. The unwinking light that meant 'action stations' threw a pale red glow over the face of the man sitting opposite. Two bulky figures waited to take our places the moment we had jumped. A dispatcher in greasy overalls stood clinging to a bulkhead with his arm raised. At the appropriate moment he would give the signal and the man on his left would jump. That meant I would be first out. Green light – the arm dropped – and I was out. A tug and a jerk as my static line took effect and I found myself drifting swiftly down under the starry night sky of Provence wondering what on earth had hit me in the eye and realizing that it was none other than my own long hair, of which I was rather proud. There had not been enough sorbo-rubber headgear to go round and although someone had offered me a helmet without padding I told them I didn't fancy breaking my neck on landing and declined. I blinked at the rapidly approaching countryside. Bathed in moonlight it looked still and peaceful, only the glow-worms of the signal lamps hinting that the darkness might conceal something other than silent homesteads. A meandering river gleamed a promise of hot afternoons, darting dragon-flies and a bobbing float . . .

'My God!' I suddenly realized, 'I'm going to get wet again.' Memories of my drowned rat act on the beach at Cannes flashed before my eyes as I tugged frantically at the shrouds in a desperate attempt to swing myself towards dry land. The Royal Air Force, for whom I'd had nothing but praise only seconds earlier, now became the target of a torrent of abuse. If only they had not been so darned expert I might have had a chance. The Americans, for example, would never have dreamed of dropping anyone from less than 1,000 feet. Generally it meant missing the landing area but at least that was preferable to being deposited in a watery grave from 600 feet. Inexorably, regardless of kicks, twists and jerks, I sped towards the shining surface praying that I would not be inextricably caught up in the cords and smothered in sodden silk. At about forty feet the capricious God who looks after subversive agents indulged his warped sense of humour by changing the 'river' into an unyielding chalk road and I landed with a bone-shaking thump in a cloud of white dust. It was one o'clock in the morning.

Automatically I began to divest myself of my 'chute and harness. Overhead I could hear the Stirling droning its way back to North Africa. Other parachutes were still descending. Splintering and crashing noises intermingled with excitable French voices on either side of the road. Horses snorted and there was a creaking of cartwheels. From behind a clump of bushes three shadowy figures appeared and without so much as 'By your leave' began to bundle up my belongings. A craggy individual in dungarees and a beret, his unshaven face lit by the glowing stub of a cigarette, asked in a matter-of-fact way 'Which one are you', and on receipt of the information told me to follow. As I trailed after him his minions disappeared with my parachute gear.

Nobody took a scrap of notice of us as we made our way across the scrub-covered landing zone with its little clumps of trees. I was at once impressed by the way in which the Resistance had grown up since the melodramatic days of 1942 when everyone was learning the business; and the difference since 1943 when the tension was at its height and the German counter-measures at their best. The operation bore all the hall-marks of the professional and I was impressed as well as relieved. Many times in the past, especially during the abortive period I had been associated with Carte, I had heard stories of strong well-armed Resistance groups, only to discover that they didn't exist. This was different. We were in business.

The sight of bustling figures transferring containers from a farm cart to a lorry parked under trees by the roadside was further proof of the efficiency of the organization.

'Well, Jean, what do you think of us, eh?' said a voice, and a grinning P-M. appeared in his shirt-sleeves round the bonnet. He was obviously delighted with himself. And not without reason. Already he had dispatched the other officers who had landed, sending them on their way with special teams of guides. All the parachute containers had landed in the dropping zone and his men were hard at work removing their contents. Now he could dispose of me too, according to the timetable he had laid down. Within half an hour of landing I was installed in the outhouse of a farm. My suitcase, which had been dropped separately with one of the container-loads, had been delivered by two excited teenagers who gaped at my British uniform. Now my instructions were to change into civilian clothes and get some sleep. P-M. announced that he would be back in the morning to pick me up, then vanished to supervise the clearing of the dropping zone.

Alone in the oil-lit hut I carefully brushed the chalk off my uniform and folded it neatly before placing it in the suitcase. Standing there in my underpants I felt sorry to see it go. To have revealed the fact that I was a British officer would probably have cost me my life two years earlier. In those days no one knew what the outcome of the war might be and a Frenchman was more likely to give away an Englishman than not. When I was on the Riviera only the Bartolis had known the truth about my origins. Everyone else had assumed that I was a Parisian. Today the more people who knew I was a British officer the safer I would be. Victory was in the air. Now it was the strange Frenchman who was in danger from a Resistance movement constantly hunting for traitors.

Regretfully stowing my case under a long wooden bench I stepped out of doors. The two youngsters who had brought my luggage were sitting on a wall chatting in low tones. When I appeared they ceased respectfully and asked if there was anything I needed. I shook my head. Somewhere in the distance the lorry was moving in low gear over the bumpy roads to preserve its precious springs. An unmistakable peasant voice was urging a horse to greater efforts, and occasionally I caught the chink of chain against cart shafts. I took a deep breath and returned indoors. I found a rough blanket that smelled of tobacco, stretched out on the bench and fell into a deep, dreamless sleep.

I was awakened about seven o'clock by the arrival of two of the 'night shift' who proceeded to clatter about lighting a stove and making coffee. They were weary after their labours but were cheerful and insisted on calling me Commandant. About two hours later the noise of a car being driven at speed made me look questioningly at my comrades but they showed no concern, merely lifting another cup from the shelf and putting the coffee pot back on the stove. Within minutes P-M. himself entered, looking as fresh as ever, seated himself at the table, accepted the proffered cup of coffee and announced that he was ready to go. My mission had begun. We were to start that very day to meet the maquis leaders.

Where or when P-M. had slept that night – if he did at all – I never found out, but he certainly showed no signs of weariness as he stepped into the powerful grey Citroën of which he was inordinately proud. No *gazogènes* for him. Only the best German petrol was good enough for P-M. and he proceeded to burn it up at a remarkable rate. Fast driving is something I have always enjoyed – as long as I do the driving myself. With P-M. at the wheel, I began to have second thoughts. Cart tracks, mountain roads, paved roads and negotiable fields were all the same to him. Many of the detours were necessary in order to avoid German posts or *milice* patrols but they could hardly have been less dangerous. In fact, as I clung to the door of the lurching, bouncing Citroën, as it tore round a series of hairpin bends I came to the conclusion that the enemy would have all their work cut out to get me before P-M. did the job for them.

Speeding through a cloud of feathers which had once been a chicken I heard with relief above the bird's dying squawk that we were to stop in the village just ahead. Hurtling into the square, P-M, jammed his foot hard on the brakes, brought the car slithering to a halt in a cloud of grit, and stepped out calmly shaking a cigarette from a packet he carried in his hip pocket. I took it gratefully, hoping that my hand would not shake, and tried to appear calm as I looked around me.

Apart from an ancient cyclist in conversation with an equally ancient lady in black there were only two tiny children playing at an open door to witness our arrival. If the car attracted their attention they didn't show it. Across the square a cat sat on a battered metal table under a faded red and white sun shade outside a bistro.

'That's it,' said P-M. and strode casually over the road. Three men were sitting at a scrubbed table inside a long, cool clean room. Two of them were in their shirt-sleeves but the third wore a suit and cap. When P-M. entered all three stood up and greeted him with a warm handshake. Without ado he introduced me as a British officer and pulled up a chair. Further handshakes all round and then the man in the cap called out. A middle-aged woman appeared from a room behind the bar and two more glasses joined the three already on the table. Pleasantries having been exchanged, it was time to get down to business. The three men, as P-M. had already told me, were the leaders of a maquis of about 200 men. They were Gaullists and completely reliable. Like all the maquis they were in need of guns, ammunition, clothes and money. It was up to me to prove that I could deliver the goods.

I soon realized, however, that there was something else I was going to have to do. After ten minutes or so of conversation, not one of the three believed that I was a British officer. My Parisian accent was too good, they said. It was perfect. It was as if three Yorkshiremen had been confronted with a man who claimed to be French and yet spoke English with a fluent Cockney accent. The very advantage which had qualified me for the job were now operating against me. P-M. was half able to resolve their doubts by pointing out that no Frenchman in his right mind would ever condescend to masquerade as an Englishman. This quaint appeal to Gallic pride was not without effect. A true Frenchman would indeed be humbling himself by insisting that he was English. It was a clever ploy but I feel that my own argument carried the day.

'Besides,' I said solemnly, 'if I were French, I would not be prepared to send you arms and supplies for nothing. I would insist on er . . . shall we say commission. *C'est juste, n'est ce pas?*'

An awkward silence fell over the company as they worked that one out. Everyone present knew just how much truth there was in my remark. They were also aware that a real Frenchman was unlikely to admit it, even to his compatriots, whereas a mad Englishman might be just fool enough to risk such an insult.

In the end, Madame behind the bar, who had followed the

heated conversation with some interest and was apparently as much part of the maquis as P-M. himself, ended the impasse with the bitter comment:

'You must be English, monsieur. If you had been French you would already have asked for a deposit on the things you are going to send.'

Immediately all the Frenchmen began speaking at once but Madame swept imperiously from the room hurling behind her a reminder that the wine had not yet been paid for.

'Ah, these women,' spluttered the man in the cap, and we shook our heads in concert at the impertinence of the weaker sex.

'Well, messieurs?' I asked when we had finished commiserating with each other.

'Ah well,' said the leader of the group, whom I gathered was the local garage owner, 'then you *are* English.'

And hands were shaken once again all round to show that I was no longer in doubt.

The rest was plain sailing. Rather like a grocer I produced my notebook from my breast pocket – where it hid the outline of my pistol, which I now felt I could safely carry. So many weapons, so much ammunition, so much money. Very good, sir, delivery should be within five days. Anything else? No: Then, good morning. Pleased to have been of service.

Sped on our way by another bout of handshaking P-M. and I returned to the car and left the village in best Brooklands style.

'Do you know, it's a strange thing, but I thought that we would have the least trouble with those chaps,' said P-M.

'Then heaven help us when we meet the rest,' I replied.

Our route now lay through much wilder country. Up winding roads and tracks we roared, scaring solitary cows by isolated homesteads. Finally, chugging up a steep incline, we were waved down by two young men in shirt sleeves and tattered trousers. Each of them carried a Sten gun in workmanlike fashion. Apparently they knew P-M. and were under orders to take him straight to their leader.

We left the car and made our way into the woods which grew thickly to the edge of the road. It was early afternoon and the shade was welcome. In the clearings the heat bounced fiercely off outcrops of grey rock. The whirring of the cicadas filled the air with incessant noise. Finally in a clearing we came upon the tallest and saddest looking man I ever saw in my life, perched on a log behind a rustic table. He was in his forties, with black hair, turning grey, and he waved mournfully as P-M. appeared. What he was sad about I never found out unless it was the shortage of rations, for he was also one of the best trenchermen I have ever come across.

Unlike our previous contacts, Monsieur Melancholy did not need convincing that I was British. He had two things on his mind. The first was lunch, which he had put off pending our arrival. Each of us was given a huge piece of cold pork, a hunk of bread and a razor sharp knife. A jug of rough red wine was placed in the middle of the table. After a number of slices of meat had disappeared down our host's long scrawny throat a suspicion of content flickered momentarily across his face and he proceeded to discuss the second thing about which he was concerned. His men, about thirty in all, were desperately in need of clothing, he said. Many of them had been in the hills for some time and were in rags. As for arms, he had enough for about half of them but very little ammunition. Fortunately food was not a problem and he cut himself another slice of pork to prove it. I got the impression that he was not so weary as he appeared, this long, thin man, and noted the neat little shelters made from branches under which his men slept secure from German observation planes.

I told him it was a pleasure to take his order and he walked the best part of the way back to the car with us still clutching a piece of pork. He waved his knife as we drove off.

The mountain maquis leader had no strong attachment to any political party, but seemed to be leaning towards the Gaullists. Of the attitude of the next maquis I was left in no doubt at all.

Communist Resistance groups were among the most difficult to deal with. Having started the war in opposition to the Allies because of the 1939 Russo-German non-aggression pact, they had changed sides in June 1941 when the Nazis attacked the Soviet Union and then, as the tide turned against Hitler, had begun to struggle for internal power in France. It was little wonder that they trusted no one and found few who would trust them.

P-M. explained to me that on no account would the Communist leader allow us to visit the area where his maquis was situated.

'We have to meet him on neutral territory,' he said. 'Unarmed.'

Neutral territory turned out to be a road across a desolate stretch of heathland. In the middle of this, at some previously agreed spot, P-M. halted our rocket-like progress, nearly catapulting me through the windscreen. Slipping my pistol from my pocket and under the seat I got out and we walked for fifty yards up the road. Suddenly a man who hadn't shaved for at least a fortnight stepped from behind a thorn bush. Five other men appeared at different points on each side of the road. Two of them had Sten guns tucked under their arms and the rest had pistols stuffed into their belts or bulging in the pockets of their jackets. Each of them wore a Tricolour arm band carrying the letters F.T.P. – *Franc-Tireur Partisan*. This time there was no handshaking. P-M. and Whiskers got down to business while the rest of the Red Guard stood and glowered at me. They were pathetically shabby and underfed.

To start with the Communist leader wanted nothing to do with me. He didn't trust the British; he didn't trust Churchill and he didn't trust me. I asked him what he had in the way of arms.

'Very little,' he replied candidly. He waved at the pistols of his followers.

How about ammunition? He shrugged.

What about money? 'None.'

Despite these shortcomings he doggedly insisted that he wanted nothing from the British.

I pointed out to him that although our countries' leaders might have different points of view, I was not a political officer but a soldier. As he was in the maquis he obviously wanted to get rid of the Germans. So did I. If he took advantage of what I had to offer he would do it very much faster than if he tried with the inadequate arms he possessed at the moment. Anyway, I said, if he didn't want arms, there were plenty of other non-Communist maquis groups who could make very good use of them.

Scrubbing at his black jowl, he looked appealing at P-M.

'How far can I trust this friend of yours, Archiduc?' he said, giving P-M. his code name.

'How far would you trust me?' asked P-M.

'With my life,' replied the Communist simply.

'Then that is how far you can trust Jean here,' he declared with an impassive face.

I could see that the man was wavering.

'If you agree to co-operate and accept delivery via Archiduc's landing ground, I will deliver enough arms for you to equip your whole maquis of 140 men within a week,' I said. 'And you'll have money for food.'

That did it. The Communist held out his hand, his companions breathed a sigh of relief at the thought of filling their empty bellies, and there were handshakes all round.

P-M. made preliminary arrangements for the Communists to carry their own supplies from the dropping zone and then we left, this time escorted back to our car by a much more friendly crew.

'Where to now?' I asked as we shot off.

'Apt,' he remarked abruptly.

Apt is the capital of the Vaucluse. It had no German garrison but patrols visited it regularly.

'What are we going to do there?'

'Listen to *La France Parlent aux Français*. What else?' he announced with some surprise. 'Your people may have work for us tonight.'

I wondered at the iron constitution of the man. I was ready to call it a day while he, who, as far as I knew, had not slept since the drop the previous night was all set to deal with another consignment of arms, and prepared to make his plans under the noses of the Germans into the bargain. P-M. did not take unnecessary risks, however. On the outskirts of the town we drove up a little lane and parked the car where it would not be conspicuous. We then walked to a small apartment which P-M. used from time to time. A young man was fiddling earnestly with a radio. The Germans took great pains to jam the B.B.C. and picking up the messages on some of the ancient receivers in use was a matter for experts. Our young friend apparently had the business down to a fine art and it was seldom that his sharp ears missed anything.

On this evening, a stream of messages was pouring out, meaningless phrases like 'Red candles are better at night' or 'White wine is best'.

Somewhere in France there was someone to whom the phrases

would not be meaningless, someone who, like ourselves, would be straining to catch every word spoken by the announcer. At the same time the persevering German radio intelligence teams would be trying to make head or tail of the mass of information which contained so much danger for them.

A stiffening attitude on behalf of the listener indicated that at least one of the messages was for us. We froze while he scribbled something down.

'The farmer with the grey beard has five eggs . . .'

P-M. beamed.

'Good. We have another drop tonight. We had better eat now. Albert will pass the word to the *chef de parachutage*.'

Albert, his sharp ears and delicate fingers having extracted the news from the radio, vanished to warn the team who controlled operations on the dropping zone that they would be needed. During the day they did their normal jobs and lived at home. In that way they avoided drawing attention to themselves and were able to slip out at night and make their way to whichever of the five landing grounds controlled by P-M. was in use.

I had further evidence of the thoroughness of P-M.'s organization that night when two large four-engined planes dropped four men for onward transmission to other maquis groups. One of the incoming agents, a weapons instructor, got his arms entangled in his parachute lines as he came down and dislocated his shoulder. Immediately he was hurried off to a place where he could receive medical attention and be sheltered until he had recovered.

'All part of the service,' said P-M.

I was glad to retire to my bench in the farmhouse and get some sleep when operations were over. It had been quite a day.

Within the next week P-M. took me to see nine more maquis, not one of which he ran himself. At each we were well received and arrangements to supply arms were completed. Generally speaking, the farther one moved into the hills the bigger the maquis became, being free from the attentions of the Germans, who tended to stay near the towns. P-M. himself had a 1,000 well-trained men in La Garde* and used a section of these to protect

* Used here to denote the area round the village of La Garde in Vaucluse; not to be confused with the department of Gard.

his landing grounds although, more often than not, the maquis on the receiving end was expected to do their own unloading. As the word spread that I kept my promises, the work of persuading the different maquis leaders to co-operate became easier. I met one of the most remarkable of these on the second day of my mission.

We had driven a considerable distance into the mountains and were in the middle of a wood when two youngsters stepped out from behind a tree and waved us down. They could not have been more than 16 years old but they were carrying Sten guns in a soldier-like fashion and were remarkably clean considering they were living in the open. It was about five in the evening and they helped us to camouflage the car before taking us on to meet their chief.

They led us up a winding track until we came to a small sloping plateau, giving a good field of fire against any surprise attack on which stood a small stone-built farmhouse. One of our escort knocked and we were ordered to enter. Inside sat a little fat man with a small pointed moustache and a goatee beard. He stood up and greeted us with a smile and a handshake and I saw that he was only about five-feet six-inches tall. Despite his lack of inches Monsieur, as all his subordinates called him, proved to be one of the finest disciplinarians I was to encounter. He had gathered to him a maquis consisting of about forty teenagers who had taken to the hills to avoid the *relève* or the *travail obligatoire*. Although a dedicated Communist, he behaved more like Baden-Powell and had the whole area under complete control. His house was absolutely spotless. As we talked a delicious smell pervaded the room. At his invitation to dine I hesitated for a moment. I wanted to know whether it was quite safe to sit down and relax in this Boy Scout atmosphere.

'Follow me, mon Commandant,' he said. And together we did the round of his posts.

He had at least a dozen sentries all beautifully placed and all on the alert. We were unable to surprise any of them. At the same time we were able to do something for their morale as Monsieur, insisted on introducing me to every one of them as a British officer. They were suitably impressed and were very polite.

Later, after we had eaten our meal, Monsieur made an excuse and left the room, saying he would be back in a minute. When he returned he brought four of his youngest recruits with him. Like a schoolteacher he lined them up at one end of the room and then raised his finger. There was a pause and then they burst into song. I am no judge of music but to me they sang beautifully. First they sang the patriotic songs of the *Résistance*. They sang the 'Marseillaise' and they sang the 'Internationale'. But they also sang the songs of an older France, the France of 1914–18 and the France of Napoleon. They sang the folk songs of the district, songs of mountains and streams, of the heroes of years before and kings long dead. As they sang, the little fat maquis leader wagged his grey goatee in time to the music and his eyes gleamed with pride. The dark eyes in the swarthy hatchet face of P-M. glistened too, but there were tears as well as pride in them. For these were boys such as he had been, sunburned, black-haired, good natured boys who should have been at college or at the *lycée*. They were boys like those I had gone to school with myself in Paris years ago, knowing the same games, reading the same books. As I watched them standing there in the little cottage room, the light shining on their youthful faces, in their smart khaki shorts and shirts, I wondered what the devil I was doing arranging to supply Sten guns, rifles and grenades to such babies. Monsieur must have read something in my face for he leaned across to me and said:

'Do not fear for them, mon Commandant. You will see. They will be all right on the day that is coming. They will be all right.'

That night, before we went to bed in the cottage, for it was too late to attempt to return to Apt, we accompanied Monsieur on his rounds. The guards had been changed – 'boys need more sleep than men' – and the new ones were as alert as the youngsters we had seen earlier. Once again I was introduced and once again they gaped at the sight of a real live British officer. I went to sleep feeling that I was in excellent hands. I hoped fervently that they would really be all right on the day that was coming.

12

THE quantity of arms and ammunition dropped to the maquis between D-Day and the landings in the south of France was staggering. I found that it was impossible to stick to the original plan for me to fly to and from North Africa to notify them of our requirements and give them situation reports. It was essential for me to remain on the spot and take the orders, then to relay them and leave the reception arrangments to P-M. To have commuted would merely have wasted valuable time.

The system for selecting dropping zones is worth recording. It was done simply by using the Carte Michelin for the particular area. After a suitable spot had been selected by ground observation, the number of the Carte Michelin plus the square number of the map would be radioed back to London. Then the R.A.F. would come over and photograph it and if they were satisfied the drop was on. The beauty of this system was that if the Germans did pick up a radio transmission the numbers were meaningless to them.

Most dropping zones were about 100 yards by 300 yards and the men who worked them developed their techniques to a fine art. Normally the R.A.F. would send over one or two planes. Four members of the reception committee with red torches would take up their positions in an 'L' formation in the centre of the zone and wait there. They had no cover. If the drop was being made by the R.A.F. you could be fairly sure that the pilot would be painstaking in his approach. Sometimes they would do as many as three runs before deciding that they were on target and at the right height.

Then, as the plane roared over at about 800 feet, its perspex glinting in the moonlight, great pale golden ghosts would glide swiftly to the ground and apparently be swallowed up. Spotting just where these parachutes landed was a key job for the watching teams. Once the planes had delivered their cargo no time could be lost in picking up the containers, manhandling them on to carts and lorries and whisking them away to isolated spots where they could be hidden and unpacked at a later date. The parachutes themselves went to make underwear for the wives and sweethearts of the reception committee.

A plane might carry a load of a dozen containers, the contents of which varied. Sometimes the emphasis was on ammunition and magazines. A load might contain 50,000 rounds and 240 magazines for Bren and Sten guns. Or it might be mixed, with half a dozen Brens, three dozen .303 Lee Enfields or American carbines, twenty-seven Stens, five pistols and forty Mills bombs – plus the rounds to go with the weapons and the detonators for the grenades. Most loads carried field dressings as well.

Bazookas and their rockets, explosives and fuses and Piat anti-tank projectors completed the regular supplies to the ever increasing armoury of the maquis. Some six-pounder anti-tank guns were also brought in, although I was never present when one was landed. Mysteriously, a Hudson once landed bringing in a solitary out-size cannon, plus a French gunner colonel to go with it, but that was dispatched to some strange maquis with a particular problem farther north.

I remembered how glad I had been to have three 'drill-purposes-only' Sten guns when I pedalled round my weapon-training classes in Nice and Cannes in the winter of 1942! It was a surprise to me to read in *S.O.E. in France* that Francis Cammaerts, a lieutenant-colonel in the French section of S.O.E., was highly critical of the service he received from Massingham when he was serving in south-eastern France. He is quoted as having described the packing as 'shocking' and reckoned that more than a fifth of the supplies dropped to him were lost because the parachutes did not open or the containers burst on hitting the ground. Cammaerts also described an 'inexcusable' incident in which a container hit a house and 'crushed the back of the mother of one of the reception committee'. These complaints were made early in 1944 but apparently resulted in no change in the quality of service.

All that I can say is that Cammaerts seems to have been singularly unfortunate. All the supplies which I asked for were delivered on time and if the R.A.F. was doing the job they landed more or less in the right spot. American pilots were apt to be more erratic, for they liked to operate at about 3,000 feet, took only one look at the spot and sent their loads on their way with the pious hope that they would land somewhere near the target. The pilot who managed to drop Christine Granville seven miles from the D.Z., set up an all-American record. Poor Christine, who was murdered in London in 1952, walked all the way to the rendezvous where, she told me, her language shocked some elderly members of the reception committee.

As far as containers falling on houses are concerned, it is impossible to see how these errors could be avoided. With the Americans it was not unusual on occasions to have containers crashing into the streets of Apt although this occurred less frequently after P-M. had sent off a strongly worded complaint. Life was made more exciting by the adoption of a new technique for increasing the flow of ammunition. After it had been pointed out to Massingham that the packing of parachutes must be taking up valuable time, experiments were tried in delivering cartons of cartridges in wicker baskets without any means of support at all. This speeded things up tremendously, especially the reactions of the reception committees who learned to cover the distance to the slit trenches in record time. The planes came in very slowly at about 300 feet, and released their contents as if they were bombs. Frequently they sounded like them, for one or two baskets went off in fine style. Drops of this nature could, of course, only be carried out in the most isolated areas.

P-M. himself had more than one narrow escape. Once he had arranged a drop on a zone in the north and was expecting to receive grenades. He stood there while the plane flew round and round without doing anything. Finally in desperation he gave the order to extinguish the torches, which were obviously not visible to the pilot, and lit three bonfires instead. Sure enough the plane made its run and the reception commitee stood gazing skywards, but they could see nothing. A violent explosion suddenly rocked the earth. Then another. And another. The grenades had been dropped in the same containers as the detonators, the parachutes had been made of black cotton instead of the usual silk, and the whole consignment went up in smoke. For two hours the grenades went on exploding, then P-M. having written off the drop as a failure, sent the reception committee home with instructions to take nothing from the site. On his way back to his own head-quarters he met three large lorries full of Germans. By amazing good luck they were all well on the right-hand side of the road and he was able to run the wheels of his car up the banked verge and get past them. Shots followed him into the night but the Germans did not bother to try to catch him. Instead they went on, searched every house in the village from top to bottom and took away three men. All three had parachute material in their homes. One, despite the fact that the Germans had arrived at 9.30 on the morning after the drop had already draped the black shrouds over the back of his bed in the most elegant Empire fashion. Another had tucked the 'chute carelessly into a cupboard. All three men paid for their negligence with their lives.

P-M.'s quick thinking when he came face to face with the German lorries was typical of him. On another occasion he rever-sed out of danger at high speed while his bodyguard, a Marseilles gangster, opened fire. Unfortunately, as he had his head turned to see where he was going, the gangster's gun-barrel gave him a nasty burn under the chin.

Even when the Germans dynamited a house where he was sleep-ing and he came crashing through the ceiling on to a badly wounded man in the room below, he remained undismayed. Al-though the injured man clung to him desperately, P-M. took care-ful aim and drove off his attackers with a pistol. The thing foremost in his mind at the time, he told me, was his British train-ing – always fire two shots at the same target. This he did with such skill that not only did he escape himself but was able to have the wounded man rescued as well.

The Germans were often singularly ignorant of maquis methods and operations and this sometimes led to ludicrous situations. One afternoon our *chef de parachutage* came back with his crew ab-solutely helpless with laughter. He had been missing for some time and we were beginning to get worried. The previous night we had received a big drop and P-M. had borrowed a large lorry from a local garage to help carry some of the stuff into hiding. Off they went at daybreak and by nine o'clock were hard at work heaving the containers into the repair shop of the garage. Suddenly a panting messenger arrived to say that six S.S. men had been seen in the area. Immediately the team took to their heels and melted into the countryside. All except the *chef*. Whether he was deaf, daring or just plain difficult is unknown to this day. But when the S.S. arrived he was still at work. On this particular day they were up to a little trick that they were very fond of in the Vaucluse area. As it was a nice dry day they were all wearing carpet slippers. Stealthily and silently they closed round the sweating *chef de parachutage*. Then they tapped him on the shoulder. 'Thank heavens you've arrived,' he said, without batting an eyelid. 'I thought I was going to have to shift this little lot myself.' And the Germans who had never seen a parachute container before, set to and helped him to store them.

One complaint I think was justified was over the poor standard of many of the Sten guns we received. Too many of them were unfinished and the vents in the barrels had not been properly drilled. Jagged bits of metal threatened to obstruct the passage of the bullet and jam the weapon. P-M. had to set up an armoury in the hills where local gunsmiths and other experts examined *all* weapons before issuing them.

One day, during this period of intensive activity, I had a visit from a good-looking blonde with brown eyes. We met in the back of the bicycle shop in Apt which P-M. used as one of his safe houses. As I had already been told that she was a courier for Circonférence a circuit some distance away led by a French officer, I asked cautiously what she wanted. Although I was sure she was genuine I had no instructions either from London or from North Africa about changing the scope of my operations.

'I have been sent to take you to the Circonférence,' she said brightly. Circonférence was an old friend of mine, Willie Wiedman, who had completed his training at my *cabanons* at Sidi Ferruch, but I did not let on.

'Oh, yes,' I replied. 'What for?'

'He wants to see you,' she continued perkily. 'He wants you to supply him with Stens.'

I looked blank.

'But I have not enough for the local maquis,' I lied.

She was not put off.

'I am sure you will be able to do something,' she said with a sugary smile.

It didn't work. I had my orders and nothing could change them, not even the blandishments of this blonde charmer.

Avoiding the issue, I asked her what her name was. When she told me it was 'Binette' it was all I could do not to burst out laughing. Whichever genius at Baker Street decided to christen this smart young thing 'Hoe' must have had a strange sense of humour. Anything less like a straight thin garden implement than this curvy creature was difficult to imagine.

'That is a stupid name, my dear,' I eventually replied. 'What's your real name.'

'Marguerite.'

'All right, that is what I'll call you.'

'And will you come with me to see Circonférence?' she demanded anxiously, as she perched on the table in the little office-cum-kitchen-cum-bicycle-repair-shop.

'Oh, I'm afraid I cannot come at the moment,' I said shaking my head. 'Tomorrow perhaps.'

In the end Marguerite (her surname was Petitjean) remained in the area for ten days trying to convince me to make the trip. She was under the impression that I was a scared new boy on my first mission and did everything in her power to assure me that I would be all right in her company. I did what I could to encourage her in this belief, which made her rage all the worse when she found out that this was my third tour of duty. She threw the best part of the bicycle shop at me and hammered on my chest with her little brown fists. Still, we were friends by the time she left, although I never did go to see Circonférence. I had orders to remain where I was for the time being. According to *S.O.E. in France* Marguerite returned to England by crossing the Pyrenees. Apart from the fact that such adventures were completely unnecessary by that time, when the Allies were overrunning, or about to overrun, France, I seem to remember kissing her goodbye before she took off in a Hudson from one of P-M.'s landing grounds.

A more sinister character who arrived in the kitchen of the bicycle shop about this time was a charming white Algerian who rejoiced in the code-name of Pioche. In French this means a pickaxe and the effect of walking into a bar and asking, 'Has anyone here seen Pickaxe?' would have been as devastating as going into a hairdressers and asking 'Is Hoe still under the drier?' I can only assume that the man who gave Pickaxe his name was influenced by his particular role in S.O.E. He specialized in assassinations and according to legend was unable to do his job properly unless he had sexual intercourse twice a day, once in the morning and once at night.

Of all the men I met, he was probably the most reckless and the luckiest. His one-man blitz on the bridges of Marseilles became a legend. P-M. had decided for some reason I can no longer recall that seven bridges in the city needed to be blown up. Pioche was given the job. Regrettably, P-M. said, he was unable to provide a suitable 'safe' house for Pioche to use before and after the mission.

It was a task that any normal man would have spent a considerable time preparing and planning before setting out. Pioche was not normal. He packed two large suitcases full of explosives and pencils, armed himself to the teeth, and caught the train. Earlier in the war men got away with this sort of thing. A member of Carte called Matthis actually convinced a Gestapo official at Nice station that P.E. was sculptor's modelling clay when his luggage was searched! There was no chance of meeting a booby like that in 1944, but Pioche counted on his luck. It held and the bridges were duly blown. Pioche, however, was far from happy when he returned.

'Never again ask me to do such a mission,' he complained. 'Never again.'

The train, apparently, had been crowded and he had soon got into conversation with a lady who had squeezed up to make room for him. Pioche was his usual charming self. The lady inquired if he had anywhere to stay in Marseilles and Pioche was delighted to accept an offer of hospitality, with all it implied, for the night. It was, in any case, magnificent cover for him to walk off the station with a local woman, and it provided him with a 'safe' house. Had the lighting of the train been a little better he might not have been so keen to accept the invitation. For once in the full light of the lady's home he realized that her make-up had been most skilfully applied.

The grey of her hair had not dimmed the sparkle of her eye and although she admitted to being a trifle over 60, she held him to the bargain they had struck on the train. Gallantly Pioche made the sacrifice and shared the lady's bed for the night. He did, however, not avail himself of her hospitality after he had carried out the demolitions. Grateful though he was for the shelter of a 'safe' house the blow to his pride was considerable.

What the 60-year-old proprietor of the bicycle shop thought of his visitors he never revealed but I know that Pioche, whose real name was Louis, puzzled him deeply. He would sniff and chew his moustache and then sniff again as if trying to weigh him up. The sniffing was understandable, for Louis liked scent and used it liberally. I wouldn't have been surprised if he had washed his clothes in it. Why it was necessary for him to shoot people when he could have smothered them by standing next to them in the lift I'll never know. But shoot people he did. And the reason for his aromatic presence in Apt was that he had just demonstrated his expertise on a particularly obnoxious Gestapo chief at Aix-en-Provence.

Unfortunately the murdered man's henchmen were promptly on the scene and actually had Louis trapped at one time until, under a smoke screen of Attar of Roses, he shot his way out of the cordon surrounding him and eventually reached Apt.

Louis was a likeable and highly entertaining companion. Just before the war he had been sent to Paris by his father with a string of horses and had sold them at a handsome profit. Unfortunately he had spent the money on himself and when war broke out deemed it safer to remain in France than return to Algiers to face the wrath of his father. Resistance work came to him quite naturally. About 30 at the time, he was five-feet ten-inches tall, athletic, and had a particularly mobile face which bore a thin white scar from temple to chin on one side. Smartly dressed in an impeccably-cut lounge suit, with expensive shoes, he doted on children and had all the patience in the world with them. He too made his exit one day via our landing ground and I was genuinely sorry to see him go. The bicycle shop never smelled the same again.

Grim confirmation of a disaster in the north filtered down during the last few days of July and the beginning of August. The maquis of the Vercors, a mountainous region near Grenoble, had tried to fight a pitched battle with the Germans on the Vaissieux plateau barely fifty miles away and had been massacred. More than 3,000 men had fought elements of three German divisions for a week. In the end, without heavy weapons, anti-tank guns or air support the inevitable had happened and they had been overrun. Prisoners were tortured, villages sacked and women raped. As an exercise in courage it was magnificent. As a lesson in maquis tactics it was deplorable. P-M. was wild when he heard the full extent of the casualties.

'The fools,' he raged. 'Why couldn't they wait. When the Americans have arrived with their big guns they can fight the pitched battles for us. Our job is to hit and run, to snipe the stragglers, trap the lorries and draw 100 Germans into the mountains chasing one man who can vanish at will.'

I said little. British officers had been among the advisers at the headquarters of the French regular colonel commanding the Vercors maquisards. I had no idea what part they played in the battle and felt it better to make no comment. Inwardly I prayed that no one would give a premature order for the rallying of our own maquis groups in Vaucluse. I had no wish to see the atrocities of the Vercors repeated.

I had just had a gruesome, first-hand opportunity to study the handiwork of German 'reprisal' tactics at close hand. At the end of a grey wet day P-M. was driving at his usual breakneck speed back to his own maquis area when a car pulled in at a cross roads and honked its horn loudly signalling us to stop.

Recognizing it as one of his own 'fleet' he halted sharply and pulled over. Two white faced young men in their early twenties hurried over.

'Bad news, I am afraid, P-M.,' said one. 'The Germans have picked up one of our youngest maquisards. He's dead. We've taken him back to the farmhouse at the dropping zone.'

P-M. literally hissed back at the man. 'How did this happen? Who was he? Where did it happen? Why was he away from the maquis?'

The story that followed was not too clear but gradually we pieced together what had happened.

The boy, who was about 17 years old, should never have left the area of the maquis. But he had a girl-friend in Apt and had decided to sneak in and see her the previous night. Somehow someone else had heard that the boy was coming and he had been betrayed and picked up by a German patrol who took him away. The Gestapo had been called. When they had finished with him they had left his body outside Apt as a warning to any men who might be considering joining the maquis. The two maquisards had discovered it as they were coming back from an authorized visit to Avignon. They had taken the body to the farmhouse at the landing-strip. P-M. had heard enough. Without a word he jumped back into the car, reversed and raced back the way we had come. A small group was standing near the door when we pulled up. As P-M. got out they made a silent lane for him. They looked sick with horror.

I followed P-M. inside and saw why. What was lying on the kitchen table was almost unrecognizable as a human being. It was like a scarecrow soaked in blood and poked full of holes. A check on the boy's wounds revealed that the Germans had pulled out his teeth, gouged out his eyes, torn off his testicles, caved in his ribs and broken one of his arms. One can only assume that they did it because the youngster refused to talk.

It is one thing to write about these things years later. It is another to look at them at the time. All I wanted to do at that moment was to get out of the hut. I felt nausea sweeping over me. But P-M. was transfixed with hatred for the men who had perpetrated such a monstrous thing. He moaned through clenched teeth, closed his eyes and gripped the table. Then he swung round out of the hut and back to the car. I followed at the jerk of his head. After muttering a few words to one of his lieutenants he drove off.

Not a word was spoken as we drove helter-skelter towards Apt through the dusk. After parking the car we made our way cautiously not to the flat but to a house owned by a friend, just in case the person who betrayed the boy to the Germans knew even more about the rest of us. That night we slept in the same bed in a room on the ground floor. The window opened on to a field which would give us a clear run should anyone come knocking at the front door, and we placed our pistols on the floor by the side of the bed before we lay down to rest. P-M., cold with grief and rage, was the first to fall asleep. I lay awake wondering what manner of men could have wreaked the havoc I had seen that day. The invasion of the south of France could not come quickly enough for me. The sooner we could use the mass of weapons that had been flown in the better.

A different P-M. greeted me early next morning. His rage had gone but there was something else in his eyes. His usually slow gait was even more deliberate. He seemed to glide rather than walk. It was no use trying to talk to him because he was not listening. Very calmly he slipped on his jacket and told me to report back to the maquis farmhouse.

'But where are you going?' I asked.

'Never mind,' he replied. 'You wait for me back at the farm. One of the boys will give you a lift.'

With that he was gone.

Obediently, and because I could think of nothing else to do, I got a lift back to the maquis farmhouse and spent a miserable day hanging around. It was not made any better by the sight of a newly dug grave at the edge of a field and a little cross which bore the legend '*Mort pour la Patrie*'.

Towards darkness P-M. returned. His car pulled up and he got out with a diabolical smile of triumph on his face.

'Well, I've got my revenge,' he said.

'What have you done,' I asked as he threw himself on the bench in the corner and stretched out, his arms behind his head.

'I've kidnapped a bitch,' he said. 'In fact, two bitches. One is the French girl-friend of the chief of the Gestapo in Avignon. The other is her mother. They're both collaborators and as I think their German friend is responsible for what happened yesterday I am going to put him through a little bit of torture. Once he learns that his lover-girl has gone he'll be frantic. Especially as I have left word for him that she has fallen into the hands of the leader of the maquis who lost a boy yesterday.'

He lit a cigarette and blew a contented puff of smoke at the ceiling.

'And we are not finished at that, dear Jean, not by a long chalk.'

More than that he would not say.

About ten o'clock the following day we were sitting at the table in the farmhouse making a list of requirements for our next drop when I heard a shout and looked out of the window. At the bottom of the steep path which led to the house four maquisards were half helping, half pushing two women towards us.

'Ah,' said P-M., 'our visitors.'

The door was opened and they were pushed in, one a tear-stained girl about 22 years old, the other a stout woman of 50, scared but slightly defiant for all that.

Both wore light summer coats over skirts and blouses. The raven black hair of the young one was curly and tousled. The mother wore her greying hair swept back tightly into a bun.

'Outside for a moment, Jean,' said P-M. and followed me shutting the door behind him.

'Well, what do you think of that couple,' he asked.

'Not very much,' I replied. 'What are you going to do with them.'

He gave me a strange, piercing look.

'There is only one thing we can do. Get rid of them.'

'What do you mean?'

'We'll have to shoot them.'

'Who is we?' I asked my throat and mouth going dry. I knew what was coming next but I hoped that he would not say it.

'You and I,' he said tonelessly, his eyes never leaving mine.

I made one last desperate plea.

'Must we do this?'

The relentless voice continued.

'Oh, yes. To start with they may escape. Secondly they will eat food we cannot spare. And thirdly they will need the attention of guards who could be doing better things. Besides, this is my revenge. Anyone can die for his country on the field of battle. You can die happily with a gun in your hand. But to die like that boy did, that is terrible. To inflict that suffering is unforgivable.'

I realized with a start that the two women were sitting at the very table on which the boy's body had lain. P-M. was indeed having his revenge.

'Anyway,' he continued suddenly, as if he had just discovered an irrefutable argument, 'that cow is several months pregnant. The child is the baby of the Gestapo chief. I don't want his bastard around.'

Thrusting his face towards me P-M. challenged: 'Well?'

Accidental Agent

Accidental
Agent

JOHN GOLDSMITH

Charles Scribner's Sons • New York

Printed in the United States of America
Library of Congress Catalog Card Number 78-158884
SBN 684-12449-1

The author before his first
mission

The author after his first
mission

Leonetti

Bartoli (taken in 1961)